GUNFIGHTER SELLING

Developing The Guns To Close The Big Ones

Vern O. White

Real Time Strategies, Inc.
Owatonna, Minnesota 55060

Published By:
   Real Time Strategies, Inc.
   Owatonna, Minnesota 55060

Printed By:
   Olympic Graphics, Inc.
   Owatonna, Minnesota 55060
   Minneapolis, Minnesota 55435

To my wife Patsy, for twenty-seven years of unwavering support and for her efforts in helping to edit this book.

To Frank, Jerry, Jerry, John, Lisa, Dick and Tom for their ideas and contributions in helping to make this book a reality.

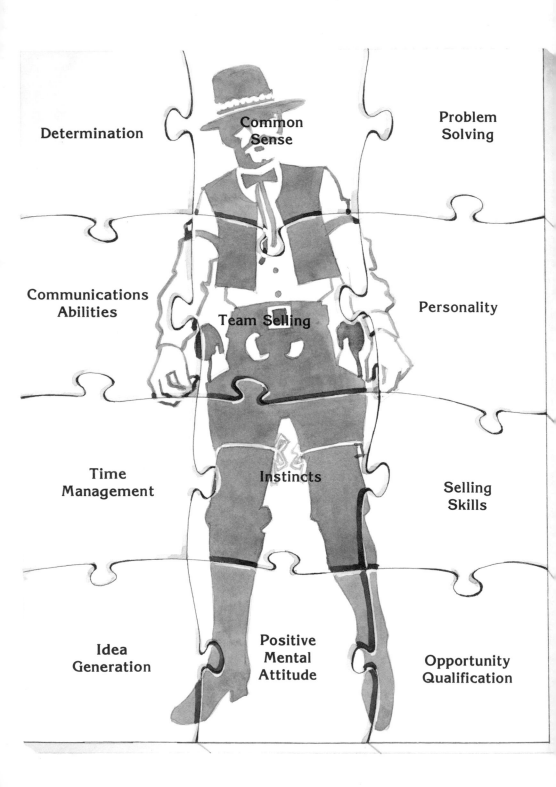

This book relates to the development of the project salesperson that possesses unique aptitudes and abilities for closing major orders and penetrating key accounts. The author refers to these individuals as "Gunfighters".

The puzzle shown on the left symbolizes the need for the salesperson to bring together all of the ingredients necessary to be successful in project sales which forms the complete picture of the "Gunfighter".

TABLE OF CONTENTS

Forward

Introduction

I. Identifying the Differences in Salespeople

II. The Gunfighter - Born or Made?

III. A Burning Desire to Succeed

IV. Maintaining a "White Hat" Code of Conduct

V. The Impact of Project Business on a Company

VI. The Match Between Gunfighter and Company

VII. Time Treats All Sales People Equally

VIII. The Bottom Line - Communicating Effectively

IX. Communication Skills - Part Two

X. If Ya Wanna Win the Game - Ya Gotta Field a Team

XI. Sales Prospecting - "There's Gold in Them Thar Hills"

XII. The Competitive Edge - Knowing Your Opponents

XIII. Secrets for Successful Sales Calls - "High Noon"

XIV. Settling Down, Moving Up or Moving On

XV. Bringing it All Together - Realizing Dreams

Appendix

Questions and Answers for the Prospective Gunfighter

Forward

This book was written for professional salespeople, by a professional salesman. It is intended to serve as an instrument for stimulating the readers thinking in areas relating to the development and honing of their selling skills.

The thoughts contained in the book are offered as one piece to the total overall development of an effective salesperson. If the reader is able to obtain four or five good ideas that will increase their selling effectiveness, then the time spent reading the book will be merited.

As a professional salesperson, I've always believed in using other peoples ideas and thoughts and adapting them to my circumstances or situations. Although most of us are able to generate original ideas, there are many more existing good ideas which can be borrowed and used at the appropriate time. I am in hopes that the reader will want to borrow some of the ideas that have worked for me during my twenty-five year career as a salesperson.

In chapter one I make distinctions between the various types of salespersons. I have come to believe that there is a certain type of salesperson that is uniquely qualified and capable of closing large dollar volume projects and penetrating new accounts or business opportunities. I refer to this type of salesperson as a "Gunfighter".

This book was written for the Gunfighter.

Introduction

There may have been a time when a gift of gab, a black leather sample case and a sense of determination were all that were needed to be successful at selling. If there were ever such a time, it has now passed.

To be successful at selling in the late 80's and early 90's, an individual must approach the profession with the same discipline and preparation as would a doctor or lawyer. When making this comparison it is important to remember that we are referring to the professional salesperson. Selling is their "life-long" chosen career field.

This transition from the "time of the peddler" to the "era of the professional salesperson" has come about as the result of many factors. The advancement of modern technology has had the most significant impact on the field of selling. In todays competitive marketplace, one thing is certain; what is now, will change. With the on-going development of new products, the life cycles of all products have been reduced significantly. In order to be successful at selling in this environment, the salesperson must be highly adaptable. At issue is not only that there is change taking place, but that the rate of change continues to accelerate.

Another significant change that can be witnessed almost daily is the number of acquisitions and mergers that are taking place between companies. These frequent changes in the complexion of a company often require that a sales force "re-orient" themselves virtually overnight. Salespeople must be able to adapt to these conditions through the development of personal selling skills that allow them to make the transition to new products and in some cases, to new markets, in relatively short periods of time.

Other factors that have significantly changed the nature of selling are:

- The increased mobility of salespeople
- Improved telecommunications systems
- Companies are becoming larger and more complex
- The average dollar size of orders has increased
- The use of computer based information systems
- Customers have become more informed
- The rapid transition to "marketing driven" companies
- In most companies, purchasing has become a science

One does not become a professional in any field without preparation. The professional athlete may be born with certain physical attributes, but only those committed to rigorous training and development rise to the top of their chosen area of competition. In the field of selling, each individual must decide if they wish to perform their sales duties as an amateur or be willing to make the commitment to the study and self-development necessary in order to become a professional.

In summary, almost every day represents a new challenge for the professional salesperson. Only those that take their personal development seriously will survive over the long term. As the size of the selling challenge becomes greater, the size of the rewards will increase proportionally.

"Everyone lives by
selling something."
Robert Louis Stevenson

CHAPTER ONE

Identifying The Differences
In Salespeople

Successful salespeople are unique individuals. It is estimated that there are twelve million individuals in the United States that earn their living by persuading others to purchase or lease their particular product or service. This represents approximately five percent of the population of our country. Needless to say, there are many different types of sales positions, and the knowledge and skill levels required of each of them is varied. It is not my intent to suggest that one type of sales is better than others. If an individual is successful in their chosen field of sales and takes their responsibility to the customer seriously, they have the potential for becoming a professional salesperson.

Industrial or "Business To Business" Selling

The focus of this book is directed to the aptitudes and skills necessary to be successful in the area of selling often referred to as industrial, commercial or "business-to-business" selling. There are an estimated 1.3 million individuals active in this type of sales activity. In this sales environment, the targeted customer may be another company, a non-profit organization, or a local, state or national governmental agency. By this definition, it eliminates consumer sales activities.

The 80/20 Rule Applied To Salespeople

A number of studies have been conducted on the relative effectiveness of salespeople. One of the most revealing studies was conducted by Jeanne and Herbert M. Greenberg based on their study of 360,000 salespeople in the United States, Canada and Western Europe. They found that. . . "approximately 20% of the salespeople account for 80% of the sales", and that "about 55% of the people holding sales positions have little or no ability to sell, while another 25% have sales ability but are attempting to sell the wrong product or service".

These findings are consistent with my own experiences in working with various types of salespeople and my observations as to their relative sales effectiveness. These opinions have been reinforced time and time again when visiting with other sales managers. Each of them are able to identify their "Star Sales Performers" and also those from which they anticipate marginal results. In one organization that I worked with that was having difficulties growing, we concluded that 12 of 19 individuals in the sales force were relatively ineffective in their sales efforts, yet had been with the company for a number of years. Changes were made and the company began to grow.

If a salesperson isn't consistently in the top half of the sales performers of a company, they should take a serious look at their choosen vocation. Ultimately they will have to stop blaming other factors such as the product, support levels, the territory, the economy, poor training, management, etc., and deal with the reality of whether or not they should be attempting to make their living as a salesperson.

The Four Types of Industrial Salespeople

In order to have some frame of reference, I like to place the various types of industrial salespeople into four categories. I call them; The Experimenter, The Average, The Farmer and The Gunfighter. Figure 1. provides a brief overview of the characteristics of each of these types of salespeople. Again, I am not attempting to cast negative dispersions on groups of individuals, but merely trying to reflect the differences that I see in various types of salespeople.

2

Figure 1.

The Four Types of Salespersons

Type of Salesperson	The Experimenter	The Average	The Farmer	The Gunfighter
% of Total Salesperson Population	50%	30%	17%	3%
Type of Sales to Which Best Suited	Working in developed territory	Non-competitive environments	Account Development - Service oriented	Account penetration - Closing big projects
Level of sales Experience	3 hours to 18 months	2 years to a lifetime	5 to 10 years minimum	10 years or more (depending on availability of mentor)
Level of commitment to sales career	Undetermined	Will stick with it until something better comes along	Lifelong	Lifelong
Level of annual income	$8,000 - $16,000	$15,000 - $35,000	$40,000 - $65,000	$50,000 and up
A company would prefer to pay them	Commission only	Small to moderate base plus commission	Mid-range base plus bonus or commission	High base plus bonus on sales & profits
They would prefer to be paid	Strong base salary	Base salary and % of sales	Mid-range base plus open-ended commission	Open-ended commission
Chances for success in sales	Low	Moderate	High	High

The Experimenter

All salespeople begin in this category. As in any other profession, the individual has to pay their dues. There are only two options open to those that are Experimenters. They can either move up to one of the other three categories or they can leave the selling profession.

There are numerous factors that influence individuals to accept sales positions. When these expectations are met, the individual often goes on to a lengthy career in sales. When they are not met, the individual becomes disillusioned and leaves the job. Examples of influences:

- The lure of the "big money"
- A high interest level in a specific product or service
- Someone sells them a "bill of goods"
- They are uncertain as to their career path
- They have significant knowledge in a market or industry
- They are attempting to emulate a successful role model
- A relative owns the company
- The first sales come easy (i.e. - insurance to a relative)
- They are often easy jobs to get (limited exposure to company)
- They are embarrassed to be "out of work"
- A desire to work in an "unstructured" environment
- The appeal to wearing nice clothes and driving a nice car.

The Average

The second largest category of salespeople are those that can squeeze out a living but whose performance is relatively marginal. They may appear to have an occasional good year which results primarily from the fact that their territories have a smaller revenue base than that of the top performers. For many reasons, this type of a salesperson usually has one good year out of every three. This is often the minimum level of performance that is required by some sales managers in order for them to hold on to their jobs. I refer to this category of salespeople as "The Average" group.

The individual in "The Average" sales group can move in three directions. They can stay in sales and earn a reasonable living, they can move on to the ranks of the Farmer or Gunfighter groups or they can select another occupation. Many who are unable to move up, chose to remain in sales for their entire careers. Some of the factors that influence their decision to remain in sales are as follows:

- They enjoy the freedom that a sales position offers
- They believe they are viewed as a professional by others
- They experience a relatively low tension level on their jobs
- They are often frugal and good personal money managers
- They are often challenged by involvement in outside activities
- They often handle rejection quite well
- They can avoid the home office culture and environment
- They are very "benefits" oriented (Insurance, vacations, etc.)
- They see themselves as "top flight" salespeople
- The money they make is better than they could do elsewhere
- They are often highly knowledgeable in a product or industry
- Occasional or frequent travel appeals to them

The Sales Professionals

The final two categories of salespeople are those that are the consistent performers in sales organizations. It is the individuals in these two groups that have earned the title of "Professional Salesperson". Although their approach to selling is significantly different, both of them are consistently successful in closing orders. They are the 20% that "make" 80% of the sales.

The Farmer Salesperson

The description of "Farmer Salesperson" is offered with a great respect for what they are able to accomplish. Their approach to selling is much like the American farmer who plants their seeds, cultivates the crop and harvests the fruits of their labor at the appropriate time.

The Farmer salesperson begins a sale by identifying a customer that has a need for their product. Getting the first order, regardless of its size, is similar to the farmer planting their seeds. The development of on-going relationships of trust and the servicing of the account can be compared to the cultivation of the land. If the salesperson is successful and the customer continues to have a need for the product, a flow of orders will result and the salesperson can harvest the fruitful crop.

The Gunfighter Salesperson

The second type of salesperson that qualifies as a professional is "The Gunfighter". This individual seeks out and pursues large contracts or attempts to penetrate new accounts which represent significant sales potential. His or her dealings with a specific customer may occur only once during their entire career but the stakes are often high and a single sale may earn the salesperson as much as other salespeople may earn in an entire year.

Like the gunfighter of the old West, this individual has a tendency to be willing to take risks that other salespeople would tend to avoid. They are often required to work on a project for extended periods of time in a highly competitive environment where success or failure is dependent on many factors. The Gunfighter salesperson thrives on the competitive challenge and views the pursuit of every order as a "shoot-out" with their competition.

It is my opinion that the skill levels required by both the Farmer and the Gunfighter are very similar. Of particular importance in all types of sales is the development of the salespersons personal communications skills. Most of the differences between the Farmer and the Gunfighter lies in their natural aptitudes and in their personalities. In short, "What type of sales environment turns them on?".

Of equal importance is the environment in which each of the two types of salespeople can work effectively. The success of many companies is dependent on being able to hire and motivate the Farmer salesperson. The Gunfighter can only be successful in certain types of companies. Much of this compatibility between Gunfighter and company is dependent on the type of management of the company and their understanding of the project business. Gunfighters have an orientation towards projects, Farmers have an orientation towards developing on-going business. The second of these is much more easy to manage and results in a much more predictable business environment.

Making Things Happen

One might wonder how 80% of the people in sales can continue to survive if they are generating only 20% of the business. The truth of the matter is that their territories do more than 20% of the business of a company, but not necessarily because of the salespersons efforts. Orders are often influenced by factors other than the salespersons efforts. Some of these factors are:

- The customer has purchased the product previously
- The customer was influenced by advertising of the product
- Exposure to the product or service at a convention
- The companys' good name in the industry
- Word of mouth by other satisfied customers
- Participation by the company in trade associations
- Customer relationships with other key company employees
- The company offers a unique "single source" technology
- Direct mail, telemarketing or other promotion programs

Those individuals in the Farmer and Gunfighter classifications "make things happen" in their sales territories. They can be transferred from a successful assignment to one that represents undeveloped territory, and they will find a way to be successful. One of the frustrations that they experience is that their sales territories are frequently reduced in size because of the volume of business they are generating. With these individuals, as the territory becomes smaller they will find a way to maintain or increase the volume of sales that they were previously achieving. When their territory size is reduced they often become frustrated with the belief that they are not being compensated fairly for their early missionary work in the territory.

Focusing on the Gunfighter

The remainder of the book will concentrate on the closing of project business and on the role of the Gunfighters. To some degree, all salespeople visualize themselves as Gunfighters. During their careers they may have opportunities to "close the big one". It is my contention that "the big ones" are most often closed by those individuals that have targeted their aptitudes, skills and energies towards the highly complex sale. It takes a special type of salesperson to be successful in this competitive arena.

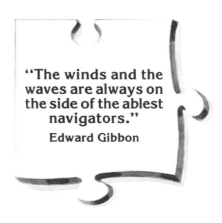

"The winds and the waves are always on the side of the ablest navigators."
Edward Gibbon

CHAPTER TWO

The Gunfighter — Born or Made?

The Gunfighter Salesperson is born with special aptitudes and spends a lifetime developing unique selling skills. Rarely does a month go by that I do not read or hear the question asked... "Is a salesperson made or born?". My most recent exposure to the question was an article in Success magazine entitled "Salespeople are Made!" by W. Clement Stone, the well known speaker and author. In this excellent article, Mr. Stone stated... "But selling is an art that can be taught".

This book relates to the Gunfighter selling, so I will sidestep the issue of whether salespeople in general are born or made and focus only on the successful project salesperson. There is no question in my mind that the Gunfighters I have worked with were blessed with certain "God given" aptitudes and natural abilities which greatly contribute to their success when selling in highly competitive environments.

Gunfighters are born with potential sales abilities. Although they may not come out of the womb with the brand of "Salesperson" on their foreheads, at some point in their life they come to recognize they have special "persuasion" abilities. Not all of the individuals that have this gift chose sales as a career path, but those that do, "have it".

Identifying These "Gifts" In An Individual

The natural abilities that a Gunfighter draws upon are often difficult to recognize, and may not be evident even to the individual until late in their careers. Intuitively they "KNOW WHAT THEY KNOW", but their strengths in these areas may need to be identified and re-inforced by someone they respect, and in whom they recognize the same special selling abilities. I am a believer that the easiest route to becoming a Gunfighter is to work for one. That manager must have "Experienced the Life" of a Gunfighter and be willing to share their knowledge with a subordinate.

It is important in a young salespersons career to recognize the difference between a "role model" and a "mentor". If you admire an individual, you may attempt to pattern your behavior and style to theirs with the hopes of emulating them. I have little confidence that this approach of following a role model will help the individual to become a better project salesperson. When a mentor relationship is developed between two individuals there is a common bond and understanding between them. The developing Gunfighter needs a sounding board that can relate to the idiosyncrasys of their selling environment.

Gunfighters Are Problem Solvers

If I were to pick one single factor that makes the Gunfighter unique from other types of salespeople, it would be that they do not sell products or services, they sell solutions to problems. They have a natural inclination to be problem solvers and are "turned on" by the challenge of meeting or exceeding a customers requirements. In recent individual interviews with ten Gunfighters, seven of them indicated that they were recognized as problem solvers by family and friends during their youth. Of interest was that many of them also saw themselves as problem generators.

Many salespeople approach a sales opportunity with a focus first on the benefits that their product offers and then try to match the features of their product to the customers requirements. The project salesperson reverses this process. They start by focusing on the problem that needs to be solved and then determine if their product will provide the solution. Once they determine that they can provide the solution, the "race is on". If they cannot provide the solution, they will inform the customer. Making a sale becomes secondary to solving the problem. It is this honest perspective that allows them to build credibility with the buyer.

They Don't Dwell On The Past

Another characteristic of the successful project salesperson is that they don't dwell on the past. They spend their time dealing with the present and planning for the future. Reminiscing or evaluating about "what could have been" is not in their nature, although they do learn from their mistakes.

I believe that it is this quality that allows them to deal with the frequent rejection a salesperson faces. They view the loss of an order that may have meant significant financial benefit to them as "all in a days work". They also spend very little time "celebrating" their successes. They direct their energies towards identifying and preparing for the next challenge. This perspective is a "state-of-mind" which is inherent in the individual. It can be "brought out" but it can't be taught.

Natural Aptitudes, Personality and Acquired Skills

The remainder of the chapter will focus on specific aptitudes, personality traits and acquired skill levels that make up the Gunfighters arsenal of selling weapons. Figure 1. provides an overview of those areas discussed.

Natural Aptitudes

Clearly the most effective method that I know of to measure an individuals natural aptitudes was designed by Mr. Johnson O'Connor in the 1920's. His research into natural inborn talents has been an ongoing program conducted by the Human Engineering Laboratory of the Johnson O'Connor Research Foundation. During the past half century, this non-profit organization has tested and evaluated over a half million individuals. They have also conducted exhaustive studies that follow the career paths of individuals after they were tested to determine their natural aptitudes.

Figure 1.

NATURAL APTITUDES

PROBLEM SOLVING
INSTINCTS
COMMON SENSE
IDEA GENERATION
ABSTRACT THINKING

PERSONALITY

SOCIALABILITY
WEARABILITY
EGO DRIVE
SHARING THE GLORY

ACQUIRED SKILLS

COMMUNICATIONS SKILLS
TIME MANAGEMENT
PERSUASION AND SELLING TECHNIQUES
TEAM SELLING TECHNIQUES
OPPORTUNITY QUALIFICATION TECHNIQUES

Ms. Margaret E. Broadley has written a book entitled. . . "Your Natural Gifts" which explains the work of the Johnson O'Connor Research Foundation. The book has a chapter devoted to the aptitudes of a salesperson. In her book, she states. . . "Those who make selling a lifetime career, who really enjoy it and are successful at it, fall into a definite aptitude pattern, a pattern that occurs only once in fifty-four persons."

During the past ten years I have used the services of Johnson O'Connor to test a number of my salespeople. If you desire additional information on their services, they have testing facilities in most of the major cities in the United States. In the following discussion the views offered are my perspective on natural aptitudes, and do not necessarily represent the position of Johnson O'Connor. My knowledge in the area of aptitudes comes only from "hands on" experience with project salespeople.

The Instincts Of A Gunfighter

I know of no test that can measure individual instincts, but I do know that successful project salespeople have a special talent or knack for sensing hidden information or conditions that may exist on a project. It is this "sense" that they draw upon to ask the right questions at the right point in time. An animal may have instincts for survival, the salesperson has instincts used when they are interfacing with other individuals.

If you watch them at work with a customer, you can sense their perception of key issues almost as if they had a special "antenna" mounted to their foreheads. They obtain information that others will miss. Later in the chapter on developing communication skills it will become evident that their insight comes from an ability to read peoples positions through their eyes. Although I believe that this ability can be developed, the person must have the inborn sensitivity.

Intuition differs from instincts. Intuition is an unconscious awareness without attention to reasoning. Some people may be more intuitive than others. I believe that a salesperson benefits more from their natural instincts than they do from intuition. Intuition is based on "feelings". Instinct is the ability to "read between the lines".

Is Common Sense Common?

In most professional occupations, common sense is an important ingredient for success. This is especially true for the project salesperson. Common sense is the ability to make sound judgements and decisions on the everyday happenings in life. The project salesperson works in a business environment where their counterparts have risen to the top of their professions. They usually know common sense, or the lack of it, when they see it.

I've had the opportunity to work with a number of individuals that I believed had all of the ingredients necessary to be successful at project selling, save one. They did not have the ability to apply practical reasoning to their daily decisions. The project salesperson must be able to prioritize the importance of events and separate the "deals" from the "big deals".

I wish I knew where common sense came from, I'd bottle it up and make a fortune selling it. George Gallup Jr. and Alec M. Gallup recently conducted a survey of 1500 individuals that had achieved a great deal of success in their lives. Their findings were published in a book entitled... "The Great American Success Story". Seventy-one percent of those surveyed saw common sense as the cornerstone to their success.

Common sense allows the salesperson to separate extraneous information from the relevant issues impacting a sale. As discussed in other parts of the book, one of the key challenges of the salesperson is the ability to sell the home office on the merits of a project and to get the support and co-operation from other employees to help to consumate the sale. Too much information places the decision makers in an "overload" condition. As Sergeant Friday used to say when he was gathering evidence on the TV series "Dragnet", "Just give me the facts".

Over the years I've come to believe that common sense can be cultivated to some degree, but that it takes a great deal of time and patience. Others would argue that you have it or you don't. I believe that if conditions exist where a mentor and a salesperson are mutually committed to each other there is some hope for improving on the common sense of the salesperson. This is especially true if the individual lacks maturity. Although some people never grow up, none of us ever stop growing if we have the desire to improve ourselves. Unfortunately, the older we get, the less willing we are to take direction or constructive criticism from others. It takes a very special relationship based on trust and respect to be open to working on areas such as common sense and maturity.

The Ability To Generate Ideas

Successful salespeople have fantastic abilities to generate ideas. This ability is used when dealing with the customer and home office personnel. Successful project salespeople always have this ability. It is of special use when they are countering a customers objections or barriers that could block a sale. Johnson O'Connor refers to this aptitude as 'Ideaphoria" and their testing measures the rate of flow of an individuals ideas.

If an individual is not naturally strong in the generation of ideas, they will find the task of selling very frustrating. In the project sales business, more than in any other type of sales, there is usually a very short "window of time" during which the sale will be won or lost. The salesperson's ability to "think fast" and identify numerous alternatives, while under pressure, is often the single factor that allows them to succeed.

Abstract Reasoning

The greater the complexity of the sale, the greater the likelihood the salesperson will have to correlate the facts presented to them in order to understand the entire buying process. This becomes much more apparent in the project business due to the number of decision makers involved in the buying process.

If a product is new or in the early phases of its introduction, the salesperson is often involved in what is referred to as "concept selling". This is the most difficult type of selling and requires an individual that is good at abstract thinking. There are fewer factors "cast in concrete", both from the prospective of the customer and from the company offering the product. Much of the communication from the customer may involve abstract ideas which will have to be visualized by the salesperson. This is the challenge accepted by the Gunfighter.

The Untypical Typical Gunfighter Personality

The personality of the Gunfighter salesperson surprisingly is nearly opposite to what people would sterotype the typical salesperson. This may be due to the fact that the Gunfighter is more of a problem solver than they are a salesperson. The problems that they attempt to solve are complex and require unique solutions. They operate in a highly competitive environment and their personality is one of the keys to their success.

Adjectives like. . . self-confident, out-going, enthusiastic, determined, motivated, etc. are common attributes which we conjure up when we think of the image projected by the successful salesperson. We often think of them as "Mr. or Ms. Personality". In my experiences with successful project salespeople, I have come to believe that many of the perceptions of a salespersons personality do not apply in the case of the Gunfighter. In the remainder of this chapter I will offer some of my perspectives on the personalities of Gunfighters that I have known.

Sociability

One might believe that in social environments the Gunfighter would be. . . "the life of the party". Their strong communications skills and their confidence in themselves would make them naturals for being the center of attraction. Almost to a person, I have noticed that the exact opposite is true. These individuals enjoy having the spotlight on them in selling situations, but they play a much more conservative role when socializing. They prefer to participate in groups in a more relaxed and less visible role.

If a salesperson has a strong outgoing personality in social environments, they are probably not a Gunfighter. This may sound opinionated, but I believe that taking this type of a personality into the project selling environment is disruptive to the "problem solving" approach to selling. The Gunfighter prefers not to be the "center of attraction", either off or on the job.

Selective Friendships

I believe that most Gunfighters prefer a few loyal friendships as opposed to the Farmer salesperson that seeks out and enjoys a broad range of friends. Although this may sound like a generalization, it appears to me to be a part of the makeup of the person that succeeds in the project business. The friendships that they form often last an entire lifetime. This is related to their sense of commitment to anything in which they decide to participate. Their marriages also tend to be long-lasting.

Wearability

In the garment business, the term wearability means quality and durability. I use the same term to define the quality of an individuals personality whose style displays actions or behavior not offensive or intimidating to other individuals. Sometimes the more we know of someone, the less comfortable we are in their presence. When strong personalities are displayed, others often feel the need to "protect their space". The Gunfighter has a personality that "wears well" with other individuals. The more you know of them, the better you like to be in their presence. Customers feel the same way about them.

Project salespeople have learned that they must spend more time listening to others and less time talking. Customers are often pleasantly surprised when they interface with the project salesperson for the first time. It is often the critical element necessary for the development of an ongoing relationship with the customer.

Control of Ego

In order for a salesperson to deal with the rejection that they must frequently face, they must have a strong sense of self-confidence. This strong self-image, if not controlled and kept in balance, can be viewed by others as "over-bearing". Salespeople are often viewed as arrogant or egotistical. Gunfighters have matured to a point where it is obvious to others that they have a strong belief in themselves but that it is an inner quality rather than something that has to be displayed to the outside world. They feel "good" about themselves for good reasons.

Sharing The Glory

The last personality trait that I wish to discuss is a willingness by the salesperson to "share the glory". Any order placed with a company by another organization is a vote of confidence and is a success for the company. In the case of a large order or the penetration of a new business opportunity, the order will be highly visible throughout the company. This type of a "victory" is usually followed with recognition for those individuals responsible for getting the order.

On occasion I have witnessed salespeople virtually running down the aisles of their companys' offices waving an order in their hands and in effect saying... "look at me, I'm a hero". It is always interesting to me to watch a Gunfighter deal with the success of obtaining a large or key order. Rarely have I seen the case where the Gunfighter wasn't quick to point out the contributions made by others in ensuring the order. Their behavior reflects not false modesty, but rather a genuine belief that it always takes more than one individual to close a major project. From my experience, the Gunfighter feels better about their role as a team leader than they do about being a star performer.

Part of the desire to share the credit for an order is a sense of fair play, but of equal or maybe greater importance is that the Gunfighter recognizes that he or she will have to count on the same team members for projects pursued in the future. They know that... "The glory of todays order will be yesterdays news tomorrow". By openly recognizing other team members contributions to getting an order, they are able to enhance their own careers by strengthening their position on future projects.

17

Acquired Skills Round Out The Individual

Over half of the book is devoted to the development of personal skill levels that ensure the success of the project salesperson. As you will have noted, I strongly believe that the Gunfighter was born with certain unique aptitudes, has a special type of personality and has a lifelong commitment to developing their personal selling skills.

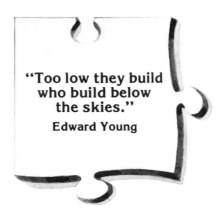

"Too low they build
who build below
the skies."
Edward Young

CHAPTER THREE

A Burning Desire to Succeed

All **salespeople have one thing in common, they have high expectations of themselves.** As in all other vocations, the intensity of an individuals desire to succeed will be the single most critical factor in determining the degree of success to be achieved. For the salesperson, success is measured by obtaining orders. To consistently obtain orders requires a very special mental attitude.

During the past twenty-five years, Mary Kay Ash has built Mary Kay Cosmetics into a $280 million organization with over 100,000 salespeople. At a recent convention in Dallas, while addressing 25,000 of her top sales performers, she stated . . . "The biggest thing is attitude. You can do anything you want to do, if you think you can. We do think we can." Although the Gunfighter works in a different sales environment, the same frame of mind or attitude that Mary Kay described is necessary for their success.

The attitude or "state of mind" of the project salesperson is especially critical to their success. In many types of sales the salesperson may be able to survive a "few bad days" and still avoid doing irreparable harm to their sales territories and sales results. If the project salesperson has one "bad day" they may jeopardize an order that they have been pursuing for months. Bad days are not acceptable.

During my career I have worked with hundreds of salespeople that had the natural aptitudes and the skills necessary for success, but lacked the fire or desire to be successful. These individuals spend their entire careers in the "average" salesperson category. On the surface they appear to have everything going for them and in a job interview they can "charm your socks off". I equate them to a Mercedes automobile with a Volkswagon engine. They look good on the surface but they have limited horsepower. They lack the drive of a gunfighter.

There are a number of words, or combination of words, used to describe that inner drive that salespeople must have in order for them to be top sales performers. I call it "an inner fire". It is one of the key ingredients that'sales managers look for when they are interviewing candidates for sales positions. Other names given to describe this "frame of mind" are:

- Enthusiasm
- Positive Mental Attitude
- Inner Drive
- Self-Motivation
- Determination
- The Fire Within
- Positive Expectancy
- Aggressiveness

Millions of dollars are spent every year in seminars and training sessions designed to add this "magical" ingredient to the salesperson. Most of these programs are directed at building self-confidence. Although many of these seminars have value, I believe that the "fire" must be a natural part of the make-up of the individual if it is to have lasting value. The gunfighter generates this fire from an inner fuel rather than from an external source. Once the source of the external fuel is removed, the fire usually dies.

The Slight Edge

There is only a slight edge of difference between the highly successful people in any field and those that settle for mediocre results. An article by Gene Emmet Clark, D.D., stated that . . . "The difference between the man of achievement and the man of mediocrity is a difference of only about two percent in study, application, interest, attention, and effort. Only about two percent separates the winner and the loser."

When "Marvelous" Marvin Hagler fought Roberto Duran for the Middleweight Boxing Championship of the World, the three judges scored the fight 144/143, 144/143 and 144/142. Hagler won by less than one percent in the scoring. When Hagler later lost his title to

Sugar Ray Leonard in 1987, he lost on a split decision with as narrow of a margin as his earlier victory. The slight edge in conditioning and mental preparation, won and lost "Marvelous" his title.

I enjoy visiting with salespeople on airplanes. Several years ago, while on a flight out of Los Angeles, I had the chance to visit with a veteran chemical salesman. During our conversation I learned that he consistently earned income in the six figure bracket by selling chemical products to key industrial users. Near the end of our flight he shared with me his secret for success. It was as follows:

"Every work day when I get up, I remind myself that I am not any smarter than my competitors, and my product is not that much better than theirs. In order to sell more than my competitors, I have to start earlier than they do in the morning and work later than they do in the afternoon."

This individual had learned the secret to gaining a slight edge over his competitors. While he had all of the skills and attitudes necessary for success, his slight edge was a mental attitude that drove him to outperform his competitive counterparts. He had "the inner fire".

Some Call it Commitment — I Call it Passion

Those project salespeople that have outstanding careers in sales have a special passion for their work. Passion is defined as ... "any intense, extreme, or over-powering emotion or feeling". That definition describes the way that gunfighters feel when they are in pursuit of a major project. The challenge is often so compelling that it becomes the dominant thought in their minds, twenty-four hours a day. Once they have had a taste of this passion or inner excitement, it is difficult for them to find the same level of challenge in other types of work. This single factor is the reason that many salespeople are "under-challenged" when they are promoted to a sales management position.

The effective salesperson is a believer that any positive change that will occur on a project must be made to happen. Their feeling of individual accountability for making something happen is best described in the "ten, two letter words" philosophy of ... "if it is to be, it is up to me". It is this sense of person accountability that intensifies the feelings of joy or disappointment when a project is won or lost. The passion of the salesperson can be compared to the doctor that is truly committed to the saving of lives or the automobile mechanic that spends a lifetime learning how to analyze the performance of a car engine by its sound and vibrations. In each case, earning a living becomes secondary to the sense of accomplishment that they experience when they are successful at their chosen professions.

Success is not a Matter of Luck

Many people look at the rewards that success brings to others and believe that the successful person has been lucky. Luck is winning the lottery, it is a game of chance. You buy a ticket and you gamble against the odds. Being successful in the project selling business is far from being a matter of luck.

In the early 1960's a sportscaster asked Maury Wills, the baseball base stealing champion, if he didn't think he had been lucky; lucky to have played for the Dodgers and lucky to have played in the warm Los Angeles climate. Maury offered the sportscaster his definition of luck . . . ''when preparation meets opportunity''. I believe that his definition of luck applies directly to the success of the project salesperson. They spend their entire careers developing themselves so that they will be prepared for the moment when they are faced with the opportunity of closing a major sale. Those that count on luck will not be prepared.

Many of my favorite verses that I have picked up over the years have unknown authors. One of my favorites relating to luck is as follows:

He worked by day, and toiled by night;
He gave up play, and some delight.
Dry books he read, new things to learn
and forged ahead, success to earn.
He plodded on, with faith and pluck,
And when he won, men called it luck.

Being Excited About What You Do

Enthusiasm is contagious. Enthusiastic people spread the feeling to people around them. Many customers like to be infected with the enthusiasm that a salesperson has for their product and the company they represent. It helps the buyer to differentiate between the prospective vendors being considered. The same enthusiasm that the salesperson displays to their customer is targeted at the decision makers in their company to ensure that they receive support for their projects.

It is a generally accepted belief that salespeople are supposed to be enthusiastic. Mr. Stan Moss, a free lance writer, conducted a survey of 44 top-ranking sales executives. In the survey Mr. Moss listed ten sales attributes and asked the executives to identify which single attribute they would focus on in making their selection to fill a sales position. Enthusiasm received twice as many first place votes as any of the other nine attributes listed.

Professional buyers are able to distinguish the difference between enthusiasm and exuberance. Exuberance is an outward display of excitement, energy and vigor. The enthusiasm shown by the project salesperson is often mellow, confident and self-assured. The professional buyer will be able to measure the level of enthusiasm in the salespersons eyes. It is generally "low key" and much more subtle than would be expected by a salesperson. This ties to my belief that the project salesperson does not fit the mold of the stereotype for the perfect salesperson. Just as they do not feel the need to be the "life of the party" in social environments, they also do not feel the need to show customers that they are constantly "up". Although enthusiasm can make a good first impression, too much of it, over an extended period of time, can wear thin on a relationship. Enthusiasm for a product or cause has to be "real" to be of any value in closing a sale.

It is a generally accepted fact that salespeople must be enthusiastic. Many customers and company employees build defense mechanisms that allow them to mentally filter out peak levels of enthusiasm displayed by a salesperson. It is important to remember that the project salesperson is interfacing with the more experienced and senior people within the customers organization and within his or her own company. The enthusiasm displayed by the project salesperson should be focused on their belief that there is a "match" between the customers needs and the product offered by the salesperson. Being enthusiastic for enthusiasm's sake is a sure way to kill a major sale.

Aggressiveness Versus Assertiveness

Over aggressiveness in a salesperson is often viewed negatively. In that aggression is viewed as "an attack", customers and other individuals build defense mechanisms to ward off the attack. A project salesperson should not "over-sell" their product and risk being thought of as overly aggressive. Their focus should be directed to solving problems, rather than attempting to force their thoughts and viewpoints on a customer. Learning to listen effectively helps to "mellow-out" tendencies towards over aggressiveness.

Assertiveness differs from aggressiveness and is a skill which can be learned. Assertiveness is also often abused in selling environments. When a person is being assertive, they are standing up for their rights. Salespeople that learn to be assertive can often appear to have the inner drive that sales managers are looking for. There are a lot of "phonies" in the world that, for short periods of time, become imposters of project salespeople. They are able to "walk the walk" and "talk the talk" of a gunfighter. In fact, they are often more convincing and persuasive than the successful project salesperson. Many sales managers are suckers for the assertive "come-on" when interviewing sales applicants. Unfortunately, they are able to "stoke their fire" for short periods of time and their enthusiasm for work, once they get the job, is in inverse ratio to the energy they expended to get the position.

Those individuals that sneak through the screening process are always in the "average" category of salespeople. They may close an occasional project, which occurs about the time they are going to get their walking papers. No matter how talented they may appear, they are almost always off of their sales quotas. They often attempt to finese their way through their work and when unsuccessful are quick to point out the inadequacies of the company. Although I am a believer of motivational techniques for getting actions from others, I know of no way to build the self-sustaining fire that must burn in the project salesperson. It is either there, or it is not.

Determination

Call it persistence, stubbornness, stick-to-it-tive-ness, or whatever, project salespeople are highly determined to be successful on any project they are pursuing. It is this persistence that makes them successful over their competitors. Sometimes they are like the bull terrier dog that has ahold of your leg. They are determined to hold on, no matter how hard you kick. I am a believer that most buyers and purchasing agents expect and prefer to work with salespeople that are slightly "pushy" and determined to get the order. Not being determined is a sign that you may not believe in your product or in its fit with the customers requirements.

The gunfighter is determined to be successful. One of my favorite verses (I understand that it was also a favorite of Sir Winston Churchill) relating to success and determination goes as follows:

Though everything looks dark and dreary, I shall succeed;
Though failure's voice speaks in my ear, I shall succeed.
I do not fear misfortune's blow and I tower with strength above
    each foe,
I stand erect because I know, I shall succeed.
The night looks long with harvest wings, but I succeed.
Out through the stars that darkness brings, but I shall succeed.
No force on earth can make me cower, because each moment and
    each hour;
    I stand affirm with strength and power, I shall succeed.

(author unknown)

The project salesperson uses their inner determination to get their fellow employees to support their projects and their customers to buy their products. They are successful because they direct their thoughts upon being successful. They are destined to be successful because of their determination to achieve success.

The Fear of Failure

Some believe that one of the most motivating factors of successful people is that they fear failure. Mike Tyson, the boxing heavyweight champion of the world is presently undefeated and is awesome in his devistation of opponents. Just before his fight with Marvis Fraser he said . . . "I have fear before every fight, I use it on my opponent. If I don't have fear, I don't fight." That same evening he went on to knock out Fraser in the first thirty seconds of the first round.

The project salesperson believes that success is never final and failure is never fatal. They balance success and failure by trimming off the emotional peaks and valleys resulting from winning or losing a project. They are not driven by the fear of failure. Although they do not like to lose, they learn how to deal with rejection and move on to the next project with optimism and enthusiasm.

The Final Ingredient - Throughness & Follow—Through

The success that the project salesperson seeks does not stop with the receipt of the order. They have a strong commitment to the success of any project in which they are involved. They know that the promises made today are commitments which have to be lived up to tomorrow. One of the key elements that the professional buyer measures in a salesperson is whether or not they are able to "deliver" on their promises. It becomes less of a question of sincerity than it is of judgement and authority to speak for the company. Also, if there are any misunderstandings after the order is placed, it is knowing whether or not the salesperson will "go-to-bat" for the customer.

My experience with Gunfighters is that the customer has little to worry about if they are dealing with a professional salesperson. In fact, most of my concerns with support and follow-through have resulted from the salesperson having a tendency to spend too much time with an account after the sale has been made. I do not mean to sound negative on this point, this is what the customer gets when dealing with the Gunfighter. Their very make-up is to "nurse" their customers and to be actively involved with each phase of the sale, including the installation and servicing of the product.

The follow-through on a project is especially important if the order is the first phase of a larger project or if on-going business is anticipated. Many project salespeople also view their customers as a part of their "sales team" and often use them not only as references, but active participants in future sales. These salespeople place heavy emphasis on "after-the-sale" support. They will often give a prospective customer the names of ten previous customers that they have dealt with and encourage the prospective customer to contact any of the names. Even if the prospective customer chooses not to contact any of the names, they are always impressed with the confidence of the salesperson in their past performance on projects.

How to Recognize "The Fire" in Salespeople

Each sales manager has their own methods to determine the inner drive that a prospective salesperson may have or not have. I like to go with previous success and references. To me, the number of projects they have successfully closed should be the contents of their resume. Other signs that may give clues to "the fire" are shown in figure 1.

Figure 1.

How to Recognize "The Fire" in a Gunfighter

- They have a lot of energy - they walk fast and talk slow

- They have a history of success in closing projects

- They are highly competitive - they don't like to lose

- They won't back away from a good fight

- They strive for success - for themselves and their team

- They are low in response to external motivation

- They are results oriented - the process is secondary

- They do not fear failure

- Once a target is identified they are tenacious in their pursuit

- They exude an inner confidence without an exterior bullishness

- In conversations they are "mellow" - when discussing a project they become "tigers".

Put it All Together and You Have "The Magic"

Just as the magician is able to pull eggs out of your ears, so is the project salesperson able to pull orders out of complex buying environments. Some call it luck, especially those salespeople that lose the order. I believe in "the magic" that a competent project salesperson can perform. It's a gift that has been fine tuned and honed into a skillful art, the art of persuasion. It all starts with the salespersons' thinking.

During a recent visit to a customers' office I noticed a plaque on the wall that I believe is suitable for closing this chapter. It reads as follows:

"Success is seldom achieved by those who contemplate the possibilities of failure."

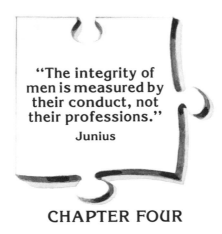

"The integrity of
men is measured by
their conduct, not
their professions."
Junius

CHAPTER FOUR

Maintaining a "White Hat"
Code of Conduct

You can't teach a salesperson how to be honorable or how to
maintain a high degree of integrity in their dealings with others.
These values are individual choices which are usually established in
the individual during their childhood. As a manager, you can "set
the tone" for your expectations, how your subordinates should deal
with your customers and provide a positive example of honesty and
integrity when dealing with others.

The project salesperson cannot survive in todays marketplace for
any extended period of time without conforming to certain principles
of conduct relating to morality. It is not my intent to preach, but rather
to share my beliefs as to what types of people are successful at closing
major projects. The sales environment the project salesperson works
in is unforgiving of dishonesty and lack of integrity.

A Nation of Liars?

Although the above heading may appear harsh, it was the title of
the lead article in the February 23, 1987 issue of U.S. News and
World Report. The seven page article dealt with what many believe
to be a decline in basic honesty. This article was but one of many
recent articles on this subject including "True Greed" in Newsweek
and "Why Cheating is on the Rise in U.S.", another U.S. News
and World Report article.

Recent developments have eroded public confidence in politicians, stock brokers, religious leaders and businessmen, including the heads of a number of major U.S. corporations which deal with defense contracts. Many so called "honest men" are spending time in jail for value judgements which they apparently took lightly when "gray area" decisions were being made. They were unwittingly willing to risk their careers and humiliate their families for the sake of success in their vocations. It is interesting to note that all of these individuals were already highly successful in their chosen fields.

I don't believe that we are a nation of liars, but we appear to be going through a period of time where many people believe that the end result of achieving business objectives justifies questionable means. In our country, trends such as these appear to be sinusoidal. For every trend, good or bad, there tends to be an opposite reaction which tends to bring conditions back to some normal level. I see this period of time as a real opportunity for those individuals that do value honesty and integrity in their dealings with others. I am a believer in the philosophy . . . "what goes around, comes around".

The Truth About Lying

Is there any basis for the belief that salespeople often tend to stretch the truth? The Stanton Corporation of Charlotte, N.C., recently gave honesty tests to 3 million individuals that were looking for employment. Busboys, dishwashers and waiters were the most honest at 88 percent. The lowest of all occupations tested was salespeople at 61 percent.

Viewing the above results, one has to wonder whether many salespeople believe that telling mistruths is part of their jobs. My purpose in sharing this information is not to draw conclusions as to the honesty of salespeople, but rather to point out the perception that others have towards the sales profession in general. It is this perception that demands that the project salesperson set themselves apart from the stereotype of the "fast talking salesperson".

Ethical Behavior

Few individuals have trouble with making value judgements on the extreme ends of the scale as to what is "right or wrong". We refer to these issues as "black or white". In the pursuit of projects, the salesperson may often be faced with moral decision on issues that may appear at the time to fall into the "gray" area of being right or wrong: It is the decisions made in these "moments of truth" that will determine the character of the salesperson. Ultimately, they face the decision of whether or not they are willing to compromise their ideals in order to strengthen their position on a project.

A number of years ago, while working as the sales manager for a large organization, I supervised an extremely bright young salesperson who called on several large accounts on the west coast. He was able to gain the confidence of the management of one of the accounts and was given many privileges, including unescorted access to their facilities. Early one morning the president of the company found the young salesman searching through his desk, obviously looking for confidential information. Needless to say, the salesperson lost his job and seriously tainted his professional reputation. This individual was successful and did not have to resort to "shady tactics". His actions betrayed the trust that had been placed in him. Why did he do it? To this day I do not fully understand his motives, but I suspect that he was caught up in his desire to be successful.

Making Value Judgements

The project salesperson is frequently exposed to situations where making value judgements may be critical to the winning or losing of an order. To be prepared for these situations when they occur, it is important that the salesperson prepare themselves ahead of time. A good sales manager can assist in this preparation.

Figure 1. provides a number of situations in which the salesperson might find themselves. Each of those examples shown will occur to most project salespeople at least once in their career. The example of a customer implying that my company would get an order if I made a monetary contribution to them personally had occurred on three occasions. In each case, million dollar orders were involved. On all three occasions I followed my own conscience, and ignored the comment. We won two of the jobs and the third project was cancelled by the customer.

I genuinely believe that once company employees begin to compromise themselves and are willing to knowingly enter into the "gray areas" of judgement, it is the beginning of the end for the company as it exists at that time. It is like a cancer that eats at the positive things in that organization.

Figure 1.

The Moment of Truth — Situations to Avoid

- If a customer implies or requests that you give them a personal monetary or object gift, change the subject and ignore the request.

- Never joke about such a request and never imply that you will think about it. Inform your management about the irregularity. Better to lose the job than to compromise your integrity.

- Do not accept privileged information prior to a competitive bid. This is especially true if it is a local, state or federal government bid.

- Never touch anything in a customer office without their approval and in their presense. What you can see is "fair game".

- Never discuss competitive bids with a competitor, especially prior to the bid. This is illegal and many people go to jail for it. It's called "price fixing".

- Obtain your competitive information by just means. Industrial espionage is wrong and unnecessary. When you are willing to do this to your competitors, who in your own company will trust you?

- Sex and business don't mix. If you try to combine the two you will always end up compromising your position and probably your career.

- Do not "pad" your expense reports. Understand company policy and adhere to it. The few dollars you can make are peanuts compared to losing managements trust and confidence.

- Do not share confidential information about one of your customers with another existing or prospective customer. If you are willing to share this type of information, can the new customer trust you?

- Avoid misrepresenting your product or company to a customer. In the project business, this can get you and your company into a lot of trouble. The stakes are too high to be playing games.

Over the years, every successful project salesperson I have worked with has had a strong personal commitment to staying on the "right" side of ethical behavior. This is not to imply that they have a "goody-two-shoes" attitude, they are not the type to point fingers of accusation at others. My belief is that their strong moral fiber contributes to their success. As a Real Time Strategist in their selling environment, they perform better because they don't have to keep track of "tangled webs" they have weaved. Their values are cornerstones to the foundation upon which they build a selling career.

A Sense of Fair Play

As I write this book I become increasingly convinced that there are many similarities between project salespeople. Their commitment to "fair play" is an example. They have certain rules under which they operate. Because of this, they are respected not only by their customers, but also by their competitors. They are always on the lookout for a fair win, not a hollow victory. In no way does this mean that they are easy targets for their competitors. They will use every legitimate trick in the book to put their product in the most favorable light.

In the heat of a competitive battle, they may see the need to go "down and dirty" as some might call it in the selling field. This is a point by point comparison between their product and that of the competition. "Fair play" is to present the facts of the comparison as the salesperson knows them to be true.

A detailed discussion of a competitors product or past performance is usually not used unless a customer has requested the information and they see the salespersons role as being helpful to inform them. It is sometimes requested by a salesperson if they believe that an order is about to be lost and they are taking a calculated risk. One has to be careful not to play the role of the "spoiler" when using these tactics. They may alienate the customer **and** the competitor and still lose the order.

The best vendor/customer relationships occur when there is a balance of fairness between both parties. A good product has a fair market value and a customer should expect to pay at that level. A company president recently expressed to me that his company was going to stop doing business with a supplier because the salesman/owner was consistently offering products at a price below what he believed to be reasonable. It offended him and made him uncomfortable with doing business with the vendor.

A successful sale should be somewhat like a love affair. Both parties should feel equally needed and wanted by the other. One wins only if the other wins. I have seen few situations in the project business where the buying organization really wanted to take advantage of a supplier. They are more often looking for a good value for their money spent through a fair business transaction. This is especially true if after-the-sale service and support are required.

Loyalty

The paragraph headings are starting to look like they were taken from the Boy Scout's pledge. Project salespeople have strong loyalties; to their customers, companys, fellow employees, business associates, families, friends, etc. They are faithful in their relationships and expect it in return. They form an allegiance with those they work with and can be counted on for loyal support.

They are willing to stick with their commitments, even when the going gets tough. Customers expect loyalty from a salesperson in the project business because they know that the salesperson may have to go to bat for them within their company. The salesperson is often as much a part of the customers team as they are their own company. Many salespeople are given unrestricted access to their customers facilities. I have seen cases where salespeople attended scheduled meetings of various groups within the customers organization. When this level of account penetration takes place, both the company and the customer want to be secure in knowing that the individual is loyal to them and will operate in their best interests.

Confidentiality

Having the wisdom to know what information can or cannot be shared with someone else is an art and a science unto itself. Some people seem to be born "blabbermouths". They are the people that you give information to when you want to be sure that it gets out to others. The project salesperson must have the judgement to separate the "no-no" from the "okay to share" information.

One rule of thumb would be that any information given by a customer should not be shared with anyone else unless there is a purpose that will benefit the customer. It actually sends chills up my spine to hear a salesperson "badmouth" one of their customers. It is a sure sign to me that they are not a professional.

As I mentioned earlier in this chapter, salespeople should be very careful what information they share between customers. I know of many salespeople that use this type of information as a "foot-in-the-door" with purchasing groups. Details like the level of the competitors purchases of a specific product can reveal the levels of their business. They can also reveal what materials go into a companys' product. I view this information to be confidential between a customer and the salesperson.

Product and business managers often are reluctant to share new product information with the sales force until it is totally ready for introduction. In the project business this is unfortunate in that the salespeople may have valuable input into the development decisions. If the salesperson is to be included into the loop of new product or market development, the individual must have shown, through past performance, that they are able to handle confidential information. When a company is investing heavily in new ventures, they must protect their investment by enforcing a policy of . . . "loose lips sink ships".

One of the factors which compels people to share sensitive information with others is a desire to appear informed. The project salesperson is already a highly informed individual and is able to share relevant information that is not sensitive or confidential.

Dealing With the Opposite Sex

Boys like girls and girls like boys. Many salespeople travel frequently or work in after-hours environments with members of the opposite sex. My comments in this section are pertinent to all salespeople, both married or single. When going to the local bar around the corner, if you're looking for something, you're probably going to find it. If in your business environment you are looking for the same thing, you also are probably going to find it. If you find it, you are going to impact your effectiveness on the job. I know of no successful salesperson that was able to mix "chasing" with business. Eventually your priorities become confused.

As the field of selling has become more sophisticated and competitive, I see fewer and fewer traveling salespeople looking for social outlets while on the road. I suspect that hotel bar revenues have fallen over the last five to ten years because those individuals that have survived in sales make better use of their time while on the road. They are either doing business in the evenings, taking a relaxing break or getting ready for the next days activities. The salesperson that spends their evening in the bar will still be in bed the next morning while they are losing their first order of the day.

Success as a Journey

Ben Sweetland wrote . . . "success is a journey, not a destination". The salesperson will experience a much more pleasant journey if they operate within a code of conduct which allows them to "stand tall" and be proud of "who" and "why" they are.

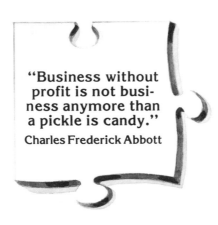

"Business without profit is not business anymore than a pickle is candy."
Charles Frederick Abbott

CHAPTER FIVE

The Impact of Project Business on a Company

Gunfighters are only as good as the companies behind them. The continued success of any project salesperson is totally dependent on their company's ability to perform to the promises or contractual agreements made during the sales pursuit and order acceptance phase of the project. In order for a company to be successful in the project business, the management must have a clear understanding of the implications of project business on a company. The very nature of the project business often places demands on various departments within the company which requires them to perform far beyond that which is normally required of them.

An understanding of these implications often results in companies choosing to avoid the pursuit of project business. Needless to say, this is not the type of an organization in which the project salesperson should be employed. The "mis-match" between a Gunfighter and a company that wishes to reject project business will result in frustration for the salesperson, sales management, top management and the ownership of a company. In this chapter we will explore the implications of the project business on a company.

One Owner's Perspective on Project Business

During a recent breakfast meeting with the owner and Chief Operating Officer of a company actively involved in the pursuit of project business, the implications of the project business on a company was discussed at length. I was especially impressed with his statement that. . . "Each project sale must be looked upon as if it were a business in itself, and that every business requires a plan". His statement that. . . "A single project can challenge every business issue of a company" was obviously based on both positive and negative experiences. He went on to share that. . . "One of my major concerns is accepting the wrong project. Even though it may represent significant revenues and profits, it can drive a company out of their target niche and have long term negative ramifications on the future of the company."

The visit intensified my belief that those companies that are successful in the project business understand this type of business and have developed safeguards to ensure they are focusing on the types of projects that are compatible with the mission of the company. This level of understanding is a mandatory requirement for any organization that is planning to hire Gunfighters.

"Front End" Qualification of Projects — A Must

One of the fundamental and most important responsibilities of the project salesperson is to qualify all prospective projects that are being pursued to ensure that they fall within the mission of the company or that they represent an area of opportunity that the company wishes to explore. The project salesperson cannot operate in a vacuum and make project pursuit decisions based only on their areas of interest, and the effect the sale would have on their sales quotas.

In many companies, the project salesperson is often viewed as a problem maker because the types of jobs they bring in are "out-of-the-ordinary". When a salesperson pre-qualifies their projects, they should gain internal support prior to spending a great deal of time on the project. Under these conditions, their projects will have a much greater chance for success once they become orders.

Selling Projects Internally

A project salesperson is as good at selling their own company on a specific opportunity as they are at selling a customer on a product. They are able to turn their persuasive skills internally and sell the company decision makers on the merits of a project they are pursuing. They are always well meaning, but occasionally self-serving.

Although few project salespeople have total control over which projects a company will aggressively pursue, they do have a great deal of influence on other company employees that they have developed as members of their selling team. The more successful they are in landing projects that are "winners" for the company, the stronger voice they have in convincing others on the merits of a new project.

The successful project salesperson is often given a great deal of latitude as to which projects they are targeting for their sales efforts. Usually, the more success they enjoy, the more rope they are given. As the projects stray further and further from the intended direction of the company they are frequently "carriers" of ulcers - they don't get them. . . they give them. . . to sales and business managers.

Not only must the project salesperson qualify projects, but so should other individuals in the company accountable for the companys' short and long term profitability. They must develop defense mechanisms that will provide a filter to the salespersons ability to "sell" internally.

Mixing "Project" and "Base" Business

One of the difficulties that companies face when a decision is made to accept a large single order is to determine how the new business will be integrated with their on-going business. As we will discuss later in the chapter, the characteristics of the project business often differ significantly from the nature of their base business.

The magnitude of this challenge is dependent on what type of business the company is currently engaged. As a general rule, I can say that the disciplines required to conduct what I refer to as "flow" business are incompatible with those required to conduct "project" business. This point will become clearer when we discuss the implications that the project business can have on a company.

Because of this incompatibility, many companies decide to separate the project business from the base business. This can be accomplished by establishing separate divisions, or in some cases, totally separate companies. This "integration" or "separation" decision can be critical to the success of both the base and the project sides of the business. In most cases, the management disciplines required to conduct an ongoing base business are drastically different than those required in the project business. To combine the two is often like walking a tightrope over Niagara Falls. One wrong step can be fatal.

The Implications of the Project Business

In the following discussion we will focus on six areas which are common characteristics of the project business. Although these conditions will vary somewhat based on the type of product and business, I have found them to be somewhat consistent in most industries in which I have been involved.

A Business of Peaks and Valleys

If a company is dependent totally on project business, they are very likely to have significant swings in their levels of incoming business and shipments revenues. The salespeople tend to be "heros" or "bums". A single order may represent a monthly, quarterly or even yearly sales quota for a salesperson.

The ramifications on the manufacturing group are equally dynamic. During the period when large orders are being produced and shipped, most departments will have to operate in an "over-load" condition. If a company staffs for these peak shipments levels, they are often over-staffed once the large orders are shipped.

If a company has a high ratio of "unforecastable" project business, they are often best served by having a flexible labor force in order to deal with the peaks and valleys. Many companies in this environment have a balance between full-time and temporary employees. The full-time staff is used to produce all of the product during the slow periods of production. Part-time and contract labor is added during the peak periods of production. The downside to this approach is that, dependent on the knowledge and skill levels required to produce the product, the quality and efficiency of the manufacturing process may decline when using other than full-time and permanent employees.

Large Projects Often Have Reduced Margins

As a general rule, the larger the size of an order a customer places with your company, the greater discount they expect from your standard pricing. This results not only from the customers expectations, but also due to the competitive environment that usually exists with the larger projects.

One of the key management issues when deciding upon prices for large projects is to be able to achieve a balance between maximizing revenues while maintaining acceptable gross margin levels. If the project in question represents incremental business over the projected base business of the company, the reduced pricing is often justified by the fact that it will absorb a portion of the fixed overhead costs of the company.

With large projects or orders, the percent gross margin levels most often decline in inverse ratio to the increase in the size of the order There is always a level in the discounting of prices where a point of diminishing returns is reached and the company is unable to discount any further. The exception to this inverse ratio rule is when a smaller company may be in a better position to discount a mid-sized project more than a larger project. Under these conditions, the larger project may absorb too great a portion of their production capabilities and their profit levels would decline to unacceptable levels.

When pricing projects, all costs should be considered. Some of the hidden costs of doing business that are often overlooked are; the cost of research and development, design, bidding, sales pursuit, commissions, royalties, engineering, tooling, advertising, promotion, freight, cost of money, service, support, warranty, insurance, inventories, bonds, etc.

The decision to include any or all of the above elements of cost go far beyond the authority and responsibility of the individuals salesperson. Many of the above costs can be waived if the project represents a ''milestone'' sale which will result in future sales at a higher margin level. Again, it is a management decision as to whether or not to price a project at a low margin as a form of investment for future sales and profits.

The Project Business - Difficult To Forecast

One of the greatest frustrations that the project business brings to an organization is the difficulty in accurately forecasting anticipated levels of business. Later in the book we will discuss the science of assigning probabilities for success to each project based on all known information about the project. The greater the number of projects being pursued, the greater the chance that the assignment of probabilities will have some value as a forecasting gauge of anticipated business.

If a company is pursuing one single large project, there are only two eventual outcomes, they will either get the business or they may lose it for one of numerous reasons. Once the order has been placed by the customer, the probability of success on the project moves either to 100% to 0%. You either got the order or didn't. The challenge is to be able to gauge the chances for success on any given project prior to receiving or losing the order.

Successful companies in the project business are able to establish a common language and level of understanding between company employees regarding the chances for success on identified projects. This area requires a great deal of teamwork and confidence between team members. This confidence can only be developed as the result of having worked on successful projects. One of the greatest assets that the project salesperson can obtain is the establishment of credibility with the key decision makers in the company.

The forecasting of project business is difficult, but not impossible. It is one of the primary skills that separates the Gunfighter from other types of salespeople. They must be able to "read" the conditions that exist on the projects they are pursuing. In assigning probabilities, they are going on record as to their chances for success on any given project. This takes a very special type of salesperson. It also requires a special type of company to support their efforts.

Increased Backlogs and Delivery Lead Times

Companies that have a higher percentage of their shipments volumes in project business usually have higher backlog levels. When a customer is anticipating the placement of a large order, they generally are looking further into the future than they may for smaller orders. They also recognize that vendors will require more time to respond to the larger orders and they will plan accordingly.

This may appear to be in contradiction to the discussion on the difficulty in forecasting project business. Once a project has become an order, it is no longer difficult to forecast. Large projects in the backlog can offer the company an opportunity to better manage their labor force and provide them improved "economies of scale" when purchasing raw materials.

Filling The Buckets

When considering the issues of having to deal with the peaks and valleys of the project business, the difficulties with forecasting and longer lead times involved, the sales organization and the management of the company must design a way to bring projects in at critical points in time. The greater the percentage of the total business that is represented by project business, the greater the need for managing the incoming business levels with future production schedules.

One of the most effective methods for achieving this balance is a method that I call "filling the buckets". It starts with an understanding and agreement on the production capacity of the company for any given period of time. Visualize each of these periods of time (i.e. - weeks, months, quarters, etc.) as empty buckets. If there are existing orders in the backlog they partially fill the buckets for the months during which they will be manufactured. If the incoming orders for the base business of the company is consistent over periods of time, this anticipated business may also fill part of the buckets. Any remaining capacity for production is represented by the unfilled portion of the bucket.

The company that is highly dependent on project business is very vulnerable when they are facing a period of empty or partially filled buckets. When you hear of companies "buying" a job, it is highly likely that they are trying to fill some empty buckets. They may be willing to accept lower margins than normal in order to at least meet their fixed operating costs and to ensure that they are able to maintain a permanent and skilled workforce.

Filling the buckets requires a team effort. First of all, each team member must know the current status of the production buckets. I've seen very large orders lost because of a salesperson promising a delivery date that a company was unable to meet. I've also seen large orders won as the result of a "window of opportunity" in the production schedule that was used by the salesperson as a lever in getting an order from a customer.

The successful project salesperson knows how to balance the need of the customer to the capacity of the plant. When they are doing their job properly, everybody wins. They are able to perform this function only when they are informed. They cannot operate in a vacuum.

43

The Need For Close Working Relationships

Later in the book we will discuss the role of the project salesperson as the quarterback of the project team. At this point in our discussion it is only important to recognize that, in order to be successful in the project business, it is essential that all departments in a company work together with the single purpose of making a project successful. I can't think of a single department in a company that doesn't play some role in the success of a project or major order.

In order for a team to work together, they must have common objectives. At some level in the organization those reporting functions that are involved in the sales pursuit, production, delivery and support activities must all tie together and be accountable to one individual. This is often the business or division manager and in many cases may be the president of the company. In order for the project salesperson to be successful over the long run, they must have an understanding of this individuals priorities for the company and what factors influence their judgements on decisions. A good sales manager will often allow the project salesperson to "end-run" them and appeal directly to this individual for support or endorsement of a project.

Additional Implications of the Project Business

Dealing with larger orders also requires that the company learn how to handle special requirements that the project may have. Examples of these are; bid bonds, performance bonds, addditional liability insurance requirements, special contracts, performance penalties, negotiations of terms, etc. In addition, the financial implications of a project can require added knowledge such as; front end payments, partial progress payments, special payment terms, bonded inventories, retainers held until resolution of problem areas, etc. Often, the financial arrangements will determine the profit level on a project. The final phase of any order is getting paid for your efforts.

Taking Projects To Enter New Markets

Many successful companies have found methods to use the project business to enter into new areas of opportunity. They view the taking on of a project as one form of their research and development efforts. These efforts are usually successful only if the decision makers have a good understanding as to the fit of the new business venture with their existing organization and with their mission for the future. You may be familiar with the Product/Market Matrix which plots the companys' existing and new products on one axis and the existing and new markets on the second axis. When accepting an order for a project, the chances for overall success are greatest when the company is offering an existing product to a market in which they are currently doing business. The company is the most vulnerable when they are offering a new product to an unfamiliar marketplace.

In Summary

If a company is highly dependent on the project business, the company management should recognize that it is one of the more difficult types of businesses to manage. It requires a great deal of teamwork and a staff of competent salespeople and internal staff to ensure that they are pursuing potentially profitable business. It is usually the industry and the nature of the product that will determine whether or not there is a "project" buying environment. Once this is understood, the company management then has two choices, they can learn how to be successful in the project business, or they can change businesses. The other possible choice is stay in the business but not understand it, which will eventually result in their having to get out of the business.

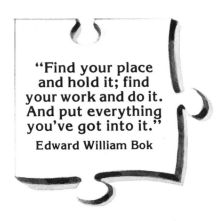

"Find your place
and hold it; find
your work and do it.
And put everything
you've got into it."
Edward William Bok

CHAPTER SIX

The Match Between
Salesperson and Company

The correct "match" between a project salesperson and a company is of paramount importance to both parties. In this chapter we will discuss the "interdependency" between the Gunfighter and the company or companies they represent. In many situations, the project salesperson may not be an actual employee of the company such as in the case of the independent manufacturers sales representative. Most of the material in the chapter is applicable to both the direct company salesperson and for those whose services are contracted.

In order to better understand the differing perspectives of the salesperson and the management of a company, the information will be divided into two sections. The first will focus on the salesperson evaluating prospective employers, the second targeted to the process that companys go through in hiring project salespeople.

Gunfighter Abilities Transverse Markets

The Gunfighters natural aptitudes, personalities, skills and selling experiences allow them the option of transversing or "cross over" to new products or markets. Most salespeople will change companys four or five times during their adult careers. I've read salesmans' resumes that listed ten or more previous employers. While not trying to be judgemental as to how many times a salesperson should change companys, my point is that there is a high probability that the project salesperson will work for more than one company during their careers.

The abilities of the Gunfighter are valuable in any selling environment. These assets are the critical elements they bring to a company, not product or industry knowledge. The specialized knowledge of a product or industry are important, but they can be mastered by the individuals that give the energy to learning a new selling environment.

A recent experience supports my belief that the project salesperson is able to change products and markets with relative ease. A project salesperson served as a territory manager for a company that was active in the education and public assembly markets. The individual had a nine year history of selling support equipment for the performing arts and had closed numerous large projects. Several years ago he elected to change jobs and took a position with a company active in the contract furniture industry, which has a totally different type of sales distribution. Within this period of time he has become their top sales performer and has increased the revenues in his assigned territory in excess of 50% in each of the past two years. He was dealing with a different product, to a new market, with a different type of distribution. Successful salespeople are successful salespeople. They can transverse markets with relative ease.

The significance of this factor is that Gunfighters and companies should not feel "trapped" in their options of seeking or filling a sales position. The Gunfighters options are unlimited, all they have to do is find a company in the project business. A company does not have to limit their search to a narrow focus within their own industry. Many would disagree with me, and they would be wrong. Its all in understanding the nature of the project business.

The Decision to Change Companys

I am a believer that project salespeople should change jobs at least every ten years. Staying with one company for too long a period tends to dull the individual and limits their exposure to different environments and methods of doing business. The longer an individual works with the same group of fellow employees, the greater the chance for "group think". You start to know what someone else is going to say before they say it.

A salesperson doesn't have to wait until they are angry or disappointed with a company in order to make a job change. Sometimes its just time to make a change. Changing companys often presents the new challenge that the individual is looking for, or should be. When the project salesperson changes companys, it is usually not for monetary reasons.

Once an individual has decided to change jobs, they should go ahead and do it. Some people anguish over this decision for years. In the meantime their performance usually starts to drop. They are unhappy and the company is displeased with their performance. I strongly advise, although I haven't always followed the advice myself, that a salesperson have another job before they quit their existing job. Companys prefer to hire people that are already employed. Also, being out of work will tempt you to accept a position that may not be ideal for you. Even if you are financially stable, Gunfighters do not like to be out of work. It is not a question of **if** you will find another job. You will. It is a question of making the right "match" with a company.

Sources for the Search

In that chapter fourteen discusses changing jobs in more detail, I will limit my comments in this area to a list of sources that can be targeted to obtain information on open sales positions. Possible sources are:

- National newspapers - Wall Street Journal
- Local newspapers - help wanted section
- Trade publications
- Customer referrals
- Networking with other salespeople
- Friends
- Direct contact with prime companys
- Convention and trade exhibit contacts
- Search firms - "Headhunters"

What to Look for in a Company

Figure 1. provides a list of some of the factors that a project salesperson should consider when considering joining a company. Although there may be other items that you might want to consider, those items shown are the key factors that will determine the match that the salesperson is looking for. When you choose a mate, one of the things you look for is compatability. So should it be with a company. Many job applicants are hesitant to ask penetrating questions about a prospective employers. Most of the questions that I have offered in Figure 1. are those that are asked during the final phase of the mating dance, certainly not during the first interview.

Figure 1.

What to Look for in a Company

- Do the "key players" understand the project business?
- Is there a long term commitment to the project business?
- What is the financial stability and profitability trends?
- Are they growth oriented? What are the three year sales forecasts?
- What were sales for past five years? Both company and territory.
- Do the heads of each department appear competent?
- Does "teamwork" appear to exist between the key players?
- Can the corporate culture be identified? Could I live in it?
- How strong is their marketing and product development groups?
- Who are their customers and how close are they to them?
- What customer base has been established in the territory.
- What is their market share? Is it growing or declining?
- Where is their product in its "life cycle" phase?
- Could I develop an emotional tie to the product?
- Do they know what they are looking for in a salesperson?
- Will they pay their successful salespeople as much as a V.P.?
- What is the compensation package? Is it "open ended"?
- Who are their competitors? Do they know how to sell against them?
- What is the revenue potential in the open territory?
- Is there an established training and orientation program?
- What sales tools have been developed? Literature, Aids, etc.
- Why did the previous salesperson leave the position?

Going to Work for a Competitor

In some fields, the trading of salespeople between competitors is quite common. My advice to the project salesperson is to avoid taking a position with a competitor, particularily if it is a "head-to-head" competitor that you have faced frequently in the marketplace. We could spend pages discussing my reasons for believeing this, but let me briefly summarize them as follows:

- If the project salesperson has been successful in team selling, they have developed an emotional tie to his or her fellow team members. By going with a "head-to-head" competitor, they must now face their "loyal" team members on the competitive battlefield.
- Loyalties are important to the Gunfighter. A significant part of their success comes from the development of "trust" relationships.
- In many cases, the customer base may remain the same as their previous position. Part of the success of the salesperson is their belief in a product and the company that they represent. It is often difficult for the Gunfighter to "switch horses".
- Last, the competitor is often hiring the individual just to obtain competitive information. The salesperson becomes a "hired gun" available to the highest bidder.

A Companys Choice — To Be Or Not To Be

Before a company hires gunfighters, they should decide if they truly wish to be in the project business. In chapter four we explored the implications of the project business on a company. Many times the nature of the product and the marketplace necessitates that the company participate in project business selling. In these cases, the company has no choice but to staff their sales organization with Gunfighters.

Promoting From Within

Occasionally a company is fortunate enough to have an individual within the organization that has product and industry knowledge and also has the aptitudes and skills necessary for success in project selling. That is, they have the abilities to go out and develop new accounts and close major projects. This is a rare happening and I would hate to have to build a sales organization in the hopes that it would occur.

Early in the book I stated that it takes from five to ten years to fully develop the project salesperson. Well managed companies are willing to invest in individuals that have the potential for project sales through training and tutoring. IBM is a good example of a company that believes in bringing salespeople that have the raw talent for project sales and mold them into an effective selling instrument.

Who Should do the Search and Selection

My advise to a company when filling a project sales position is to have the key individuals meet and agree they are looking for a Gunfighter. They may use different words to describe them, but they are looking for that unique individual that is capable of closing new accounts and is able to consistently ''get the order'' on complex sales projects. Once this is agreed to by; personnel, sales management and general management your search can begin. Hiring a project sales-person is equivalent to the hiring of a vice president in importance to the company.

The Screening Process

Although I run the risk of alienating every personnel or human resources manager in the country, the worst mistake that a company can make is to have a member of the human resources staff do the initial screening for a project sales position. Although they may be skilled at interviewing, they aren't very good at selling. The project salesperson is a hot and rare commodity. At the first interview, you have to do more than just identify them, you have to be able to ''sell'' them on your company. Human resource staff members can screen the application forms and be involved with the final interviews, but they should not conduct initial screening interviews.

The task of screening applicants should fall upon the territory sales manager or company sales manager to which the successful applicant will report. Needless to say, this is a tedious job. While filling a project sales position in California, I once had to go through over eighty applications and ended up hiring someone I had already known. The key to the screening process by the sales manager is to be able to recognize early on in the interview that you are face to face with a Gunfighter. If this type of applicant is not sold during that first visit on your product, company and the opportunity that the position holds for the right individual, the probability for your being able to sign him or her on to your sales staff drops significantly. There has to be at least the start of a common bond established at that first meeting in order for the process of hiring to be successful.

A good example of this early chemistry in the relationship between two strangers, the applicant and the interviewer, occurred while I was attempting to fill a project sales position in Chicago. Having just started the search process, I had interviewed one candidate and made contact by telephone with a second candidate who lived about seventy miles south of Chicago. One page of the candidates resume was missing and therefore I was questioning him on his project sales experience. Early on in the conversation I realized that I was also being interviewed and realized that this person was not just looking for a job, he was searching for a specific opportunity. I ended up canceling my other appointments and driving the seventy miles to Normal, Illinois in order to learn more about the applicant. On the drive down, I put on my sales hat. Within the first half hour I knew that he was the man for the job. Within two days, once references were made, an offer of employment was extended. Eight years later this individual is still the best project sales person employed by that company, with million dollar plus sales made to the Chicago Board of Trade and the Mercantile Exchange Board. The bond established at that first meeting continues to be strong today.

Finding Gunfighters is a Tough Job

Unfortunately for sales managers, just as there is a limited supply of outstanding quarterbacks in the National Football League, there is also a limited supply of proven Gunfighter salespeople. The acquisition costs are usually high in both cases and sometimes the past accomplishments of an individual represented the highpoint in their career. This is not to say that hiring proven veterans is a poor risk, but that their sales performance record should be only one of many areas considered.

Raiding a Competitor

Many companies look first to the staff of their competitors to fill a sales position. In addition to having a "ready made" salesperson on the firing line, they may also gain competitive knowledge that may be of great importance if dealing with a head-to-head competitor.

Although I can't generalize and say that it is always wrong for a company to attempt to entice away the competitors best salespeople, I can say that if I am filling a project sales position I am very careful if I am considering someone in a competitive firm. Each situation is a little bit different depending on factors such as; company size, industry size, product technology levels, geographic assignment of the sales position and the criticalness of filling the position. If your company profits are hemorrhaging because of marginal or low new orders being generated, you do what you have to do, within ethical limitations.

What to Look for in a Gunfighter

If you need the salesperson to be "on-line" immediately, always go with a proven performer. Again, this can be compared somewhat to the professional sports organization that strengthens their team by signing someone from another team with a proven performance record. In the selling field, those individuals that have been successful for one company will usually be successful for other companies. There are those that would say - "If a company is looking for a Gunfighter, why not hire a proven Gunfighter?"

Throughout the book we have reviewed the characteristics of a Gunfighter. A brief overview of the make-up of the Gunfighter is as follows:

- They have the natural aptitudes for selling
- They have a Gunfighters personality
- They have the "fire within"
- They have developed their selling skills
- They are good communicators

The biggest challenge in hiring project salespeople is to weed out the phonies. Only someone that has been, or is, currently a Gunfighter can recognize a Gunfighter. All of the above five characteristics are judgemental issues.

In chapter five we reviewed the internal characteristics of a typical company that is engaged in the type of project business which is comprised of large dollar size orders. This match between the company and the individual project salesperson is critical if both of them are to be successful. If the project salesperson is too strong or too weak for the capabilities of the company or if the company is unable to deliver the quality of product or service that the salesperson sells, then the relationship between the two will be shortlived. More than any other type of sales, there has to be a "match" between the individual project salesperson and the company that hires his or her services.

"To choose time is to save time."
Francis Bacon

CHAPTER SEVEN

Time Treats All Salespeople Equally

Time is one of the few "equalizers" of salespeople. Aptitudes, skills and experience may vary between individuals, but each have exactly the same amount of time to utilize - 1440 minutes each day, seven days per week. Although we can choose what we do with our time, none of us has any control on its rate of passage.

We have discussed a number of factors that separate the "winners" from the "losers" in project selling. The management of their time ranks high on the project salespersons list of "musts" in order to be successful. The management of time is a skill that can be developed and improved upon. It is often taken for granted as the individual develops their skills in other areas. An understanding of time management can be the "slight edge" that a salesperson gains over their competitors.

In his book, "The Effective Executive", Peter Drucker stated . . . "until a manager learns to manage his time he will not manage anything, because time is the framework within which everything else gets done."

Effectiveness Versus Efficiency

Busy people are not necessarily successful. Many people that appear to be constantly "on the move", are actually covering very little ground. A number of years ago a sales manager friend, Rex Hause, shared with me his perspective on the difference between efficiency and effectiveness. He stated that efficiency is "doing things right" and effectiveness is "doing the right things". Over the years I have come to believe that this is a fundamental concept which must be understood if an individual is going to be successful in any profession. You can be efficient without being effective.

People that are efficient are constantly busy doing things that, on the surface, appear to be necessary. They are often more concerned with the process of doing things than they are with the end results. The efficient salesperson may make five sales calls per day, but little thought is given to what is being accomplished during each of the calls. Efficient salespeople are also those that usually spend a great deal of time doing dilegence to paperwork requirements and are always timely in their submittals to the home office.

The "effective" project salesperson spends their time almost totally on those activities that help them to identify and close a major project or penetrate a key account. They are less interested in the number of sales calls they make and focus on "quality" sales calls. This can be a dangerous thought pattern for the salesperson that is not a proven Gunfighter, in that it can and will be used as an excuse for not aggressively pursuing sales opportunities. Focusing on "quality" sales calls is only a valid concept if major orders are being received.

Being realistic, there are duties or activities other than direct selling that are the responsibility of the salesperson, but many of them are often extraneous. The Gunfighter must focus on those activities that will immediately or ultimately influence sales. As my sales manager friend, Rex, would say ... "that's doing the right things".

Project Salespeople Have More Freedom

In most types of sales, the salespersons activities in calling on accounts are monitored closely and their sales results are reviewed on a daily and weekly basis. There is frequent contact between the salesperson and the sales manager. Once a salesperson has a proven ability to be a Gunfighter, the manager often gives them a very loose rein and allows them to determine their own priorities.

This "freedom" in the management of their time requires that they be "self disciplined" in the allocation of available time. During the remainder of this chapter we will focus on some "tricks of the trade" I have observed in other Gunfighters who have learned to utilize their time effectively.

Success, Contentment and Happiness

Success, contentment and happiness are each a state of mind that is measured or determined individually. All three are attitudes, and we control our attitudes. In order to be a "well-rounded" person, a level of harmony, or balance, must exist between these three "states of mind" which we all search for in life.

If the project salesperson places all of their emphasis on attaining success on their jobs, they may find little contentment or happiness in life. If they place too much emphasis on contentment, they may lack the "drive" necessary for success. If an individual seeks only happiness, they may reach a point in their lives when they are not pleased with their personal level of accomplishment and contribution.

The successful project salespeople that I have known have this healthy "balance" between these three states of mind. When one of the areas gets "out-of-balance" they seem to loose their equilibrium. As I mention before in the book, the project salesperson has a need for an objective "sounding board" for their ideas and feelings. This can be a spouse, a boss or any other individual that has a sincere interest in their well being. It usually takes years to develop this type of relationship.

The allocation of time is certainly one of the critical factors which brings about a balance between the three. I can remember the expression from when I was growing up . . . "all work and no play, makes Jack a dull boy". If a salesperson is "overly driven", they have little chance to be content and happy. They may be successful, but the success will feel shallow. The salesperson must know what they want to do with their lives. They must develop both personal and business goals or priorities. Once they place their "total lives" in perspective, they will be able to make better utilization of their time.

A Tendency Towards "Overworking"

The project salesperson is driven by the challenge of their work. During a physical examination a number of years ago, my doctor told me to "slow down". I explained to him . . . "the thrill of the chase" that a salesperson experiences. He replied . . . "yes, but you don't have to be thrilled all of the time". While pursuing major projects, salespeople tend to have a sense of euphoria. When one project is closed, they are eager to tackle the next challenge waiting around the corner.

Project salespeople often build a backlog of unused vacation time. In companies that place a lid on the amount of vacation time that can be accumulated, they are frequently in jeopardy of losing the time. Their perspective is much like that of the owner of a small business, they believe that if they are away from their jobs, business is being lost. This is not always a healthy perspective.

Project salespeople have a difficult time forgetting about the project or projects they are pursuing. They may be at a symphony concert enjoying the music, but if a large project is about to "come down", they are thinking about more than Bach's third movement. They may delight in the music, but often are also exploring "strategic alternatives" for active projects being pursued.

This is not to imply that they are "all consumed". If they are married they are often fortunate to have a spouse that will "bring them back to earth" when they are over-absorbed. The spouse usually understands their passion for selling, but will tolerate their compulsiveness only to the point where it begins to distrupt the other parts of their lives.

Managing Decisions Versus Managing Time

How often have you heard the expression ... "there's just not enough time in the day"? In truth, having thirty hour days would not help most of us to accomplish more. If an individual is behind in their work, there is more often a need to be able to prioritize the tasks than there is a requirement for more time.

In project selling, deciding upon the priorities and avoiding those activities that consume time but bring about little results, requires a constant evaluation process. If the salesperson decides to lay in the sun and relax, that's okay, we all need breaks from our work. When they decide they are going to work, they should allocate their time to those areas that will influence sales.

Avoiding Activity Traps That Devour Time

I've often thought that it is just as important for a salesperson to decide where they "won't" spend their time as it is where they "will". I would estimate that the average project salesperson spends less than twenty-five percent of their work week meeting "face-to-face" with the customer. The remainder of their time is spend in preparation, travel, telephone calls, written communications, meetings, conventions, etc.

Figure 1. provides a list of some of the "time wasters" that can absorb significant amounts of the salespersons time. Learning how to identify and avoid these "activity traps" will allow the salesperson more time to focus on their priority activities.

Figure 1.

Project Salesperson "Time Wasters"

- The pursuit of low probability projects
- Ineffective planning of activities
- Leaving schedules open for unanticipated events
- Doing work which could be delegated
- Poorly organized travel itineraries
- Lack of availability of the salesperson to others
- Disorganized filing systems
- Excess time spent on "getting organized"
- Focusing on "pleasant" versus "meaningful" tasks
- Not utilizing "odd" times in their schedules
- Focusing on the past rather than present and future
- Avoiding or delaying the unpleasant tasks
- Involvement in unproductive meetings
- Poor utilization of "in-house" staff

Avoiding the Pursuit of Low Probability Projects

The project salesperson should spend most of their time moving projects through their "selling phases". Their challenge in each phase of a project is to increase the probability of getting an order. If the probability for success is not increasing in each phase, they should give serious consideration to dropping the pursuit of the project. Their time may be better spent elsewhere. Each salesperson and manager have their own thoughts as to the phases of a project. The seven phases of a project that I follow are:

1. Identification
2. Qualification
3. Sales Pursuit
4. Closing
5. Delivery
6. Payment
7. After-the-sale support

Most of the salespersons time and energies are spent during the sales pursuit phase. As we will discuss in the chapter on sales prospecting, it is absolutely critical that the salesperson qualify each project throughly before they decide to actively pursue the project. There are many factors that will determine the salespersons chances of success on a project. They begin with questions as fundamental as ... "does the customer really intend to purchase a product?" We will address the art and science of assigning the project probabilities later in the book. Figure 2. provides a list of some of the factors that should be considered when deciding on the merits of pursuing a project.

Most of the information in Figure 2. can be obtained in several telephone calls or one visit to the customers facilities. Saying "no" to the pursuit of a project is often the most difficult decision to make. Those that never say "no" to the pursuit of a project will not be successful in project selling. Like Don Quiote, they will spend their time ... "chasing windmills".

Figure 2.

Factors to Consider When Allocating Time to a Project

- Is the project funded?
- What is the estimated size of the project?
- Is there a preferred supplier? Who is it?
- Who can I expect as competitors?
- Does my product meet the requirements?
- What is the timetable for each phase?
- What are the opportunities and risks?
- Have we had previous experience with the customer?
- Who are the decision makers?
- Does it fit within our company mission?
- How much time will the project require?
- How will the pursuit impact other projects?
- On what factors will the selection be made?
- Does the opportunity represent future business?

Planning the Work and Working the Plan

The starting point for time management is being able to recognize what one hopes to accomplish. Once the salespersons objectives have been determined, they can prepare an action plan for accomplishing their goals. The plan is the overall guide that helps the salesperson keep on the right path in the allocation of their time. The plan must include the establishment of priorities on which to focus their attention. It should also identify those activities that should be avoided.

"Prioritizing" is as Simple as A-B-C

There are many techniques for the assigning of priorities, the one I like best is the "A-B-C technique". Visualize three buckets labeled A, B or C. As tasks become apparent, mentally place each of the tasks in one of three buckets. In the ''A'' bucket place all the tasks which are critical to your immediate and future success. The tasks that are important, but not critical, should be placed in the ''B'' bucket. The tasks that probably should be done but have relatively little consequence if left undone, should be dumped in bucket ''C''.

In the project selling business, the salesperson must focus on the tasks in buckets ''A'' and ''B''. Bucket ''A'' tasks receive top priority in that most of them relate directly to a customer. When the salesperson is in pursuit of a major project, all other work tasks become secondary. The tasks in bucket ''C'' should be accomplished during the ''odd'' or ''in-between times''. When you do focus on the ''C's'', make your decisions quickly. Many people have a tendency to work on the ''C'' tasks first because they are easier to accomplish and they give the individual instant gratification. These individuals come from the ranks of the ''efficient''.

The Scheduling of Time

Each salesperson should maintain a pocket calendar that they keep with them at all times. All appointments and deadlines should be documented in the calendar along with personal commitments, vacations, birthdays, meetings, conventions, bid dates, etc. This helps the salesperson to avoid conflicts and utilize their time in the most effective manner. It also helps them to ''feel organized''.

The salesperson should establish an activity plan for at least a two week ''window of time''. Although their schedule may not be totally filled, major activities should be scheduled. They should identify which projects they will be working on and which cities they will be in. Their priorities should be established for the period and they should know exactly what they want to accomplish.

Many salespeople feel the need to keep some ''open time'' in their schedules in order to deal with unanticipated events. In the project business this is certain disaster. Plan for a full workload. If events take place that have a higher priority than those scheduled, re-arrange the schedule. Open time in a schedule for the project salesperson is usually wasted time.

Using the "Odd" or "In-between" Times

The salesperson often spends a great deal of time in lobbies, on airplanes or in hotel rooms in the evenings. These are excellent times to work on the "B" and "C" tasks. It's amazing how many memos or trip reports can be written during a several hour plane flight. Using, or not using this time becomes a habit. If the salesperson doesn't utilize the odd times of their day, they will have to allocate a portion of the "productive" time of the day to accomplish them. I view these tasks as a nuisance but necessary.

Being "In Touch" or Available

The project salesperson should never be out of reach for a period of greater than two hours unless they are on vacation. When they are on vacation, their responsibilities are delegated to someone else. It is interesting to me that the effective salesperson is always the easiest to reach at unannounced times. Sometimes it takes two days to track down the highly efficient, but usually ineffective, salesperson.

The Gunfighter salesperson leaves tracks. Major projects can change direction on a daily or hourly basis and when they do, the timely involvement of the salesperson is critical. Even though they may travel extensively, they use a number of methods to maintain contact with their customers and counterparts in the company. If they work out of their home, an answering machine or service is a must. When traveling, they keep in frequent contact with their spouse, boss, secretary, switchboard operator, team members, etc. They provide their itinerary in advance to these individuals, including telephone numbers and the times they will be at various locations. This may seem like an "over-kill", but if a major project is saved, it is well worth the effort.

Starting Each Day with "Vigor"

There is an old proverb that reads . . . "as the first hour of the day goes, so goes the day". The salesperson that accomplished meaningful tasks during the first hour has set the pattern for the remainder of the day. A positive attitude is a must for good time management. It starts with recognizing that time is valuable and there must be a plan for managing it.

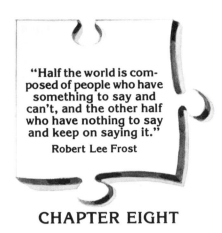

"Half the world is com-
posed of people who have
something to say and
can't, and the other half
who have nothing to say
and keep on saying it."
Robert Lee Frost

CHAPTER EIGHT

The Bottom Line -
Communicating Effectively

People buy from people. Certainly the product being purchased
is important to the customer, but it is the confidence generated by
the salesperson that "makes" a sale. The ability to communicate with
others effectively is the single most important skill that can be
developed by a salesperson. If an apprentice salesperson were to focus
on the one area of growth that would have the greatest impact on
their career, it would be in the development of communications skills.

I consider communications skills so important in project selling
that my original plans were to write the entire book on the subject.
Once I began writing, I decided that communications skills needed
to be placed within the framework of the "total development" of
the project salesperson. The next two chapters will focus on communications skills.

The Ability to Communicate

The ability to communicate effectively with others is often referred
to as ... "the greatest art in all human affairs". Those that believe
this ability to exchange information is a natural "gift" tend to take
communications skills for granted. While natural abilities vary between
individuals, good communicators work at acquiring knowledge that
helps them to skillfully apply their natural talents. Raw talent by itself
is wasted if it is not developed and applied effectively.

Within each of us lies tremendous potential for improving our communications skills. Those that focus on the development of these skills always reap huge rewards. The more accomplished an individual becomes in communications, the more they understand and appreciate its importance in project selling.

Purchasing Requires Making Value Judgements

Most buying decisions are made on the value of the product, not on its price. Establishing the value of a product requires a judgement by the customer. Those customer employees purchasing goods for large projects are usually the more experienced and competent staff members. They have proven their ability to make accurate judgement calls and are assigned the responsibility for making the major purchases.

In the entire history of the universe, only one living organism has been given the ability to make judgements - the human being. Each of us have biases, opinions, differing perspectives, predjudices, etc. The project salesperson must measure and appraise each individual involved with the buying process and select the message and media which will convince the customer that their product offers the greatest value over other products. If the buying decision is to be made on price alone, it should be pursued by an order taker, not a project salesperson. The project salesperson uses their communications skills to sell value.

The Five Vehicles of Communications

Often the media used to convey a message is as crucial as the message itself. In the remainder of this chapter and the following chapter we will discuss "the five vehicles of communications". They represent the methods used by the salesperson to achieve an interchange of ideas. They are:

- Speaking (one-on-one and public)
- Listening (one-on-one and group)
- Writing (letters, memos, notes)
- Reading (for business and pleasure)
- Body Language (non-verbal communications)

My objective in these two chapters is to stimulate the salespersons interest in the development of communications skills. The focus will be on those areas which relate to the work environment of the project salesperson, although most of the skills discussed also relate to other situations.

The importance of working on all five vehicles of communications is that the skills developed in each of them are inter-related. When the salesperson develops skills in one of the five, they become more effective in the other four. Learning how to be a better listener can help the individual to be a more effective speaker. Becoming a better speaker can improve ones ability to express themselves on paper. In fact, some of my most effective written communications are prepared when I imagine that I am giving a speech on the subject. I find that I make my points much stronger and the memo or letter tends to be shorter. This is often carried to the point where I find myself making hand gestures during the preparation of an important written document.

Verbal Communications

Understanding the link between "talker" and "listener" is fundamental to becoming an effective verbal communicator. The project salesperson is provided many opportunities to speak. In fact, the image of the typical salesperson is that they are "talkers". The effective salesperson learns how to balance the ratio between speaking and listening.

To be successful at verbal communications, one must display an aura of being at ease with other people. This applies when speaking on the telephone, visiting one-on-one, participating in a meeting or addressing a group. By first learning to relax while interfacing with others, the individual is able to be more candid, open and honest. Most people would prefer a spontaneous exchange of information as opposed to a "canned" presentation. This "comfort level" can help to defuse negative environments and can open doors for the salesperson that would normally be closed.

Communicating One-on-One

Exchanging words is easy. Communicating persuasively is a challenge. Those who are effective "one-on-one" communicators draw on many techniques to emphasize their thoughts and the depth of their convictions. They are able to learn as much as they teach.

Conversations are either spontaneous or planned. When they are unplanned and happen as a chance meeting, they have the same potential for accomplishment as those that are carefully planned. The project salesperson should have a clear understanding of what they wish to accomplish in a conversation, particularily when interfacing with a customer. All subjects discussed should fit into an overall pattern which helps the salesperson to accomplish their objective, which is to make sales.

Organizing for a "Face-to-Face" Visit

Prior to the actual interface, the salesperson should determine exactly what information they wish to give and to receive. Having an audience with a customer is a privilege that other suppliers may not be granted and should never be taken lightly.

The salesperson should make a list of the key points that they want to make during the visit and the information they wish to learn. This list should be made several days before the meeting and reviewed an hour before the actual interface. The list contains the answer to the question . . . "what do I want to accomplish at this meeting?". It should be committed to memory and also brought to the meeting to be used as a reference.

A Healthy Balance Between Listening and Talking

One of the most important factors in becoming a good one-on-one communicator is to be able to distinguish when you should be talking and when you should be listening. People that have tendencies to talk too much or too little are often perceived as "shallow" and are rarely taken seriously. Those that talk too much are so infatuated with themselves and their world that they speak to hear themselves. They have little sensitivity to other peoples interests. They pollute the air with words that fall on deaf ears. People with tendencies to speak too little are often boring and appear to be insecure when around others. In selling there must be a healthy balance between speaking and listening.

Talking with customers requires a special discipline. It is not a contest of personal wills attempting to overpower the other individual. In a positive interchange of information, the role of teacher and student switches back and forth between the salesperson and the customer. The customer instructs the salesperson on their problem, the salesperson informs the customer on their solution. You can't learn when you are talking and you can't teach when you are listening.

Maintaining Eye Contact

When interfacing directly with another individual, the salesperson should use his or her eyes as a means to both collect information and to give signals to direct the conversation. The "eyes" offer a great deal of information about the opinions and feelings of the other individual. The listeners' eyes should be used as an instrument to reveal his or her interest level and reactions to what is being said.

Whenever I am meeting with a prospective customer, I decide prior to the meeting that I will let my eyes reveal how strongly I believe in my product, and that I am genuinely interested in understanding the problem the customer is trying to solve. I am a believer in . . . "if they don't trust your eyes, they won't trust your words". I would rather say fewer words and have good eye contact, than to say exactly the right words but have poor eye contact.

Can eye contact be learned? You betcha! It starts with the salesperson recognizing the "power" of being a disciplined "reader of eyes and eyebrows". Yes, eyebrows. If you've never thought about eyebrows as a sender of messages, look in the mirror and try to display: anger, surprise, confusion and boredom using only your eyebrows. See what I mean? It takes years of study to be highly effective in this technique, but the benefits begin the very first time you use it.

The eyes of an individual mirror the interest level that they have in a conversation, the eyebrows signal a persons reactions or feelings about what is being said to them. The combination of the two provide a "gauge" to the sensitive salesperson that helps to determine the effectiveness of the sales presentation.

The Number One Fear - Speaking in Public

Year after year, the number one fear expressed by Americans in national polls is their fear of speaking in public. It is consistently ranked higher than the fear of death, heights, loss of job, etc. This fear of speaking in public results from a concern by most individuals that they will be judged harshly if their message is ineffective. Few people wish to look like a fool. Show me a person that doesn't have some degree of fear when speaking in public, and I'll show you a person that doesn't care what other people think of them.

The effective speaker learns how to control the anxiety that can build within them when addressing a group. The individual that experiences no anxiety when before a group is taking their responsibility as a speaker too lightly. We will address the subject of managing this anxiety later in the chapter.

Practice Makes Perfect

Aristotle said . . . "if you want to learn to play the flute, you've got to play the flute". If an individual wishes to be a good public speaker, he or she will have to gain experience by speaking in public. The more an individual speaks in public, with some study, the better speaker they will become.

During one point in my career I was giving nearly two hundred speeches each year. Frequently someone would come up from the audience following a speech and say something like . . . "I'd give anything to be able to speak in public like you". My response was always the same . . . "start by speaking before one group . . . then another . . . then another".

Each of us has the potential for improving our speaking abilities. Like any other skill, it must be developed if it is to happen. Those that wish to become more effective speakers must seek both knowledge and experience. All libraries have a section of books relating to public speaking. These books relate not only to the techniques for improving communications skills, but also provide subject matter for speeches.

Two Basic Rules for Public Speaking

Although there are probably hundreds of guidelines or secrets for effective public speaking, I believe that there are two basic rules which must be followed. If the speaker violates either one or both of them, both the speaker and the audience will be disappointed with the outcome of the talk. The rules are simple:

Rule Number One: Say something worth saying
Rule Number Two: Know your audience

If a speaker is not an expert in their subject matter, they will have little to share with the audience. If they have a great deal of knowledge in an area that has little or no interest to the audience, their words will fall on deaf ears. Both conditions, expertise and interest, must exist in order for good communications to take place.

Most of us are knowledgeable in a number of areas. It may relate to our work, hobbies, community, special areas of interest, etc. In all fields, experts become experts by focusing on a few areas of interest. Such is true with good public speakers, they limit their talks to those subjects in which they are knowledgeable. On many occasions I have been asked to speak on a subject I knew little about. I always decline the invitation and refer them to an expert on the subject.

Knowing the audience is of equal importance to having something worth saying. Their age, sex, reason for being together, mutual areas of interest, life styles, occupations, etc. are some of the "common denominators" which may exist in an audience. What might be absolutely right to say to one group may be totally wrong to present to another. It is of utmost importance for the speaker to know their audience.

Know What You Want to Accomplish

A speaker should know specifically the reasons for speaking to a group. Although there are many different reasons why people are asked to speak, most talks fall into one of three basic categories. These three types of speeches can be used independently or can include a combination of any of the three. They are:

- An appeal for a specific action
- To inform the group on a specific topic
- To entertain the audience

Most of the talks given by a salesperson fall into the first two categories. The results of the effectiveness of the talk are measured in terms of whether they convince the audience to support their cause or if they were able to enlighten them. The ability of a good speaker to persuade an audience to support his or her cause is like weaving a magic spell. Those that possess this ability have a crystal clear understanding of their mission.

Preparing for a Talk

If the speaker is already knowledgeable in the subject matter of the talk, the difficult part of the preparation is already accomplished. The speaker must select from their knowledge base that information they wish to convey to the audience. Many inexperienced speakers become overly involved with gathering too much information and become obsessed with obtaining that last piece of relevant material. The search for material shouldn't begin until the speaker knows what areas they want to cover in the speech.

Many speakers overly prepare and end up with too much information. As a speech or talk gets longer, the "punch" of the talk diminishes. The speaker should know "what they are talking about" and "what they want to say".

The Use of Notes During the Talk

Each speaker must determine for themselves if they wish to use reference notes during their presentation. I always recommend that notes be used by a speaker, particularily by those with relatively little experience. I believe that the use of notes has a "calming effect" on most speakers. If you like, call it a "crutch". It has been my experience that most speakers that talk without notes tend to speak longer and say less.

On the other hand, nearly everyone dislikes a speech where the speaker reads nearly verbatim from their notes. Unless scientific data or highly detailed information is being shared, never take a "word for word" text of a speech to the podium. Many speakers like to use 3 x 5 inch index cards containing the main points of their talk. Over the years I have gotten used to using business size envelopes with the flap sealed. They fit nicely into my suit coat pocket and I can get a great deal of information on them. I only have to use two or three envelopes for an entire speech.

In preparing reference notes, first determine what you want to say in the talk. Then include only the major points in your notes, arranged in sequence that they are to be presented. Underline those points that you wish to emphasize. Organize the material into three parts; the opening, the message and the close.

Structuring the Speech to Control Timing

The framework that I use when preparing a talk is; "tell em what you're gonna tell em, tell em, and tell em what ya told em". These three phases of a talk can be viewed as the opening, the message and the close. Many speakers become inamoured with the message and often speak far too long. By structuring the contents into these three sections, the speaker has greater flexibility in managing the length of the talk. Good speakers allow the audience to determine the length of the talk. The speaker reacts to the audience. The audience sends their message through their attentiveness.

If the speaker starts to lose their attention, they should attempt to revitalize them or move quickly to the close. The less accustomed the speaker is in addressing a group, the shorter should be the presentation. I've witnessed hundreds of presentations where the audience stopped listening before the speaker stopped talking. Audiences have relatively short attention spans.

Checking Out the Facilities

The preparation for a talk can often be in vain if the facility where the talk is being given is inadequate. Although facilities and equipment details are prearranged by those responsible for the program, the speaker should check them out prior to the talk. Some of the factors that should be reviewed are:

- Is the room suitable for the intended purpose?
- Will there be distractions during the presentation?
- Is there a public address system? How well does it work?
- How long is the total program? Where do you fit?
- Is the necessary audio/visual equipment available?
- Do you know how to operate the A/V equipment?
- Is there lighting available at the podium?

On the day of the presentation, always arrive thirty minutes before the start of the program to "set the scene" in your mind. A complete "audit" of the environment should be conducted by the speaker. Some things may not be able to be changed, but at least the speaker can adjust.

Stay Flexible

The best laid plans of "mice and men" often change. The speaker should always be flexible and be willing to modify their talk based on the circumstances facing them. If you've prepared a twenty minute talk and the room environment is totally wrong, you may wish to reduce the talk to five or ten minutes. If you are speaking to a large group and the sound system isn't working, there is little sense in continuing the talk.

Once several years ago in California, I was asked to give a two hour evening seminar to three hundred people. Upon my arrival I learned that the bar had been open for an hour and everyone was thoroughly enjoying themselves. After a lengthy program it was my time to speak. The total presentation was less than ten minutes with an open invitation extended to any interested parties to meet at another time.

Be Yourself

To be an effective speaker the individual must have a healthy self-image. Don't attempt to copy another speakers style. To be a good speaker, one doesn't have to be funny, nor for that matter, dynamic. The best speakers are sincere and reflect enthusiasm for their subject. The audience will first measure the credibility of the speaker and then the validity of their message. The speaker that attempts to be someone that they are not will fail the "credibility test". Better to be yourself and less dynamic than to attempt to be someone else and not be credible.

Establishing Rapport Early

The first few moments of a talk are the most critical. Not only must the speaker capture the audiences attention, they must be able to establish a bond between themselves and the audience. There must be a level of "harmony" between the "talker" and the "listeners".

One of the most effective methods to establish rapport is to identify common backgrounds, interests, similar thinking, etc. Some rapport can be established during the introduction of the speaker. Introductions should be used to build upon the credibility of the speaker with the audience. After the introduction, the speaker is on their own to further develop the relationship.

Some speakers use humor to develop rapport with an audience. It is often used to "break the ice" and place the audience at ease. To use humor, a speaker must be relaxed and have a special sense of timing. The humor should have some tie to the message of the talk. Humor is easier to use if the speaker is well known and relates to the audience.

One of my "rapport" building techniques is to establish and maintain eye contact with everyone in the room, including those at the head table and the food servers. Eye contact places the speaker in control. It helps to hold the audiences' attention and provides feedback on their reactions to the talk. It can be used effectively with both large and small groups.

Using Nervousness as Your Ally

A speaker should know that the "jitters" can provide the adrenaline they need to create the aura of energy needed for a speech. All good speakers are nervous before, during and after their presentation. The disciplined speaker learns how to orchestrate the nervousness into a powerful ally. When nervous, the speaker can feel the adrenaline building in their body which results in an increase in the heart rate and blood pressure. When this occurs, the speaker makes a "fight" or "flight" decision. Few speakers have the option of "flight" so they stay and "fight". They reaffirm to themselves that they are committed and in control.

The nervousness of a speaker is usually not visible to the audience unless there are obvious signs of tension. Audiences like to listen to speakers that are in control. The good speaker manages their nervousness and converts it into enthusiasm for their subject.

Using Hand Gestures and Body Language

If hand gestures are comfortable for the speaker they should be used, but only if they are natural movements. The body shouldn't be forced to do something that isn't a comfortable link between the limbs and the mind. Hand gestures and body language can help to emphasize key points in a talk. Hand gestures should be in harmony with the words being spoken. Good speakers often practice their hand gestures in front of a mirror when preparing for an important talk.

Some experienced speakers venture away from the podium during the course of a talk. When used effectively, it can help to establish closer contact with the audience and can burn off some of the speakers nervous energy. It has greater application for seminars and longer presentations. It should be ventured only when it is natural for both the speaker and the audience.

Avoid leaning on the podium or shifting body weight from one leg to the other. Stand straight and square with the audience. Any movement of the body should not distract from the verbal message.

In Summary

The ability to speak effectively, both one-on-one and in public, is one of the most respected and envied attributes of an individual. It can be not only a powerful selling tool, but it also helps the salesperson to maintain a healthy self-image.

In the next chapter we will discuss communications at meetings, the use of the telephone as a valuable tool and the four remaining vehicles of communications which are: listening, writing, reading and body language.

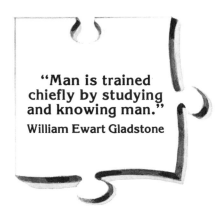

"Man is trained chiefly by studying and knowing man."
William Ewart Gladstone

CHAPTER NINE

Communications Skills — Part Two

The previous chapter introduced the five vehicles for communications (talking, listening, writing, reading and body language) and discussed one-on-one communications and public speaking. One of the key points in the chapter is that the skills learned in any of the five communications methods also improves the individuals' ability to communicate in the other four areas.

In this chapter we will focus on effective listening, writing, reading and understanding body language. Following the discussion on listening is several paragraphs relating to participation at meetings and using the telephone as a sales tool. I have included these topics because I believe they are a part of the total development of the salespersons' communications skills. Also, both of the areas require an understanding of the balance between listening and speaking.

Learning to Listen

Who would ever think that an individual would have to work at being a good listener? It's just a matter of paying attention, right? Well, that's part of it, but it is only a starting point. For the salesperson, learning how to listen is as important as learning how to talk. Many successful salespeople would argue that it is even more important.

Each and every one of the project salespeople that I have had the opportunity to work with were "excellent" listeners. Listening is an absolute necessary requirement for success in project selling. If the salesperson doesn't clearly understand the customers problem, how will they ever come up with the right solution?

Listening is a Discipline

Listening not only requires discipline, it is a discipline. It requires systematic training and adherence to certain rules. Most project salespeople get this training through experience rather than through a formal training program. Unfortunately, this takes years and does not provide the individual with a framework of understanding which allows them to pass on the techniques to other individuals.

Effective listening courses are available and are becoming increasingly more popular, although they are still not widely attended. We tend to take our listening skills for granted. It is one of the communications skill areas which can greatly accelerate the career of a young salesperson.

Listening Skills Apply to Many Environments

We most often think of using our listening skills when we are in direct interface with another individual. The same listening skills apply when we are: listening to a speech, participating in a meeting, using the telephone, or listening to the television or radio. The primary difference is that when engaged in these types of listening, the listener has little or no control over influencing the speaker.

The key to effective listening is to learn to listen for meaning. A good listener is able to "read between the lines" as they hear the speakers message. Good listening starts with having a genuine interest in what the other individual is saying. If there is no interest in the subject matter, attempt to cut the conversation or meeting as short as possible.

Guidelines for Listening

The first giant hurtle to cross in becoming a better listener is to recognize that it is an area of personal development that requires cognizance. Once an individual decides to become a better listener, they can participate in a seminar, read articles or books on the subject, or work towards teaching themselves to be a better listener.

It is especially important that the project salesperson be a good listener. Figure 1. provides a list of "guidelines for listening" when interfacing with a customer. Many of these same techniques apply to situations other than sales.

Figure 1.

Fourteen Guidelines for Listening to Customers

- Establish rapport
- Put the customer at ease
- Make a conscious effort to listen
- Place yourself in the customers shoes
- Let the customer know you are listening
- Avoid distractions - focus on the customer
- Use body language to respond without interrupting
- Ask questions to direct the conversation - then listen
- Provide feedback - "this is what I hear you saying"
- Make notes on key points - read back to customer
- If you disagree - say so, but be diplomatic
- Control emotions - avoid negative responses
- Make responses short and to the point
- Ask for information - then listen

Creating a Permissive Environment

One of the keys to effective listening is to create an environment which allows the individual you are visiting with to relax. The project salesperson must be able to put the customer at ease in order for them to "open up" on their requirements. The effective listener grants permission for the other individual to talk. This may appear to be a subtle point, but it is part of the technique used by the salesperson during the early phases of a project which encourages the customer to talk by creating a permissive environment.

One of the tricks to help create this environment is to provide feedback to the speaker that indicates that there is genuine interest in their viewpoints and that additional information is desired. This encouragement of the customer to talk is provided by brief comments and through the use of body language.

Using Body Language to Improve Listening

We use more than our ears to listen. We use our eyes and bodies as instruments for better listening. Our eyes should be focused on the speaker. They measure the conviction of the words or thoughts being shared, by reading the body language of the speaker. In the previous chapter, we discussed the eyes and the eyebrows of individuals sending signals of feelings and opinions. If the listener uses only their ears, they are not receiving the total message.

The listeners' expressions and body posture provide feedback to the speaker. The use of body language can reinforce a speakers position on an issue or question a speakers point without interrupting their talking. It can also be used to show that the listener wants more information on a specific point. The use of body language in selling environments will be discussed later in this chapter.

Meetings as a Means of Communications

Meetings require both talking and listening skills. Although often necessary, meetings are frequently a waste of time due to poor planning and loose management of them. Meetings are usually intended to share information or to make decisions. Each individual must decide their role in a meeting. If some measureable value is not achieved by each individual in the meeting, they should not be in attendance.

Prior to scheduling or attending a meeting, I always ask myself two questions. First . . . "is the meeting necessary?" and second . . . "do I have to be there?". Additional factors to consider when scheduling or attending a meeting are shown in figure 2.

Figure 2.

Questions to Ask Prior to a Meeting

- Is the meeting really necessary?
- Is it an informative or decision making meeting?
- If informative, what information will be shared?
- If decisions need to be made, what are they?
- What individuals should attend the meeting? Why?
- Is the timing of the meeting critical? Why?
- What information will be required? Who will bring it?
- Who is responsible for organizing and conducting it?
- Where and when will the meeting be held?
- Who are the key players at the meeting?
- How much time is allocated for the meeting?
- Is there special equipment required for the meeting?
- Is the meeting more important than other priorities?
- How can the number of people in attendance be minimized?

Once the above questions can be answered, the individual can decide if his or her attendance at the meeting is necessary. Some of the guidelines that I follow when deciding whether or not to attend a meeting are as follows:

- Is the purpose of the meeting important to me?
- What is my vested interest in the outcome of the meeting?
- Are there any "hidden agendas"?
- How long will the meeting take?
- How does it rank with other priorities?
- Will I be there to "give" or "get"?

Getting the Most Out of Meetings

If an individuals attendance at a meeting is required, they should ensure that they are spending the time wisely. One individual never has total control over a meeting, but each participant has some influence over the direction of a meeting. The best contribution that all parties can make is to stick to the issues or intended purpose of the meeting and make it as short as possible.

Each individual should work on listening more than talking. Meetings, particularly small groups, are one of the easiest environments for people to share their opinions, on both relevant and irrelevant issues. When not talking, the time should be spent understanding the position of those talking. Also, measure the reactions of the other participants to what is being said. Determine the intensity of the opinions. Who is lobbying for what? What are the participants motives? What frustration levels exist? How are the "decision makers" reacting to the discussion?

If a meeting becomes ineffective, find a way to leave the meeting. If it is a "boss imposed" meeting, stay, but concentrate your thinking on other areas more important to you. This may be a good time for the project salesperson to strategize on key projects. Make notes on your thoughts for future reference. Don't try to hide your activities, but make sure they are business related. You are just doing your job.

Each individual can help to keep the meeting short by stating only their key points. Participants should avoid repeating themselves. If you grow impatient with the progress of a meeting, show it. If you feel strongly about an issue, state your position but avoid arguing. Use the same skills of persuasion that you direct to customers, or be prepared to change your mind if others present a stronger case.

Using the Telephone as a Sales Tool

The telephone is the only communications device that can provide instant contact with a customer at a moments notice. When used properly it is one of the most effective tools in the salespersons arsenal of weapons. The project salesperson uses the telephone in every phase of a project, including: identification, qualification, sales pursuit, closing and after the sale support.

In project selling, the telephone is probably utilized most effectively when it is used to determine the status of a project. In that the timing of sales calls and sales pursuit activities are so critical in project selling, the salesperson must keep a close "pulse" of the status of a project. The telephone serves this purpose beautifully. Some of the advantages of using the telephone over other methods of contact with the customer are shown in figure 3.

Figure 3.

Advantages of Using the Telephone in Selling

- Provides instant access to the customer
- Time saving device for measuring status of a project
- Cost saving method - 1/200th of a direct sales call
- Provides a two-way dialogue
- Simple way to display continued interest in project
- Written scripts and backup information can be used
- Provides instant feedback on interest levels
- Allows the salesperson to move projects through their phases
- Inability to contact a customer is a "message" in itself
- Often contact can be made to those normally "inaccessible"
- It is often preferred by customers over a direct visit
- Valuable tool to re-confirm upcoming events

Getting by the Screen

Most buyers and purchasing managers are inundated with incoming telephone calls from prospective vendors. Often their calls are qualified or screened by the telephone operator, a secretary or an administrative assistant to filter out unwanted calls. The first task of the salesperson is to get past this barrier.

The salesperson that attempts to bully or force their way past the screen is on a certain course of failure. The most effective approach is to win them over and they will eventually become your ally. If they are a "trusted screen", they usually have a strong relationship with their boss or the individual whose calls they are screening. I always take the time to develop relationships with these individuals. If I show patience and respect for them, they will treat me with respect.

Unless you know the screen quite well, never share the purpose of the call. This allows them to qualify the call and reject it if it falls within the guidelines of instructions given to them. Always stress the importance of "getting through" to the desired party. Often it takes three or four calls to establish a relationship with a screen. Be gentle and let them know that you understand the role they are playing. Be as interested in talking to them as you are their boss. Always thank them when they are helpful. Treat them with professional courtesy.

Preparing for the Call

Prior to making the call, write down everything that you hope to accomplish. Unless the customer is rude, never hang up until you have accomplished the objective. One objective may be to determine if you should spend any time on the account or project. Learning this is an accomplishment in itself. Some of the items that I usually include on my checklist are:

- Who is the individual that I wish to talk to?
- Will there be a screen? Do I know them?
- How will I get by the screen?
- If the individual is not available should I leave my name?
- What are the specific purposes of the call?
- What will I use as the opener?
- What will I use to draw them into a conversation?
- What new information can I share to justify the call?
- What information will I ask for?
- What reasons will I give to make a follow-up call?

Although the above process may appear to be an "over-kill", the project salesperson is often setting the stage for million dollar sales. Every contact with the customer is important. Use whatever techniques that are comfortable for you, but always have a plan when making a telephone call.

The Conversation

The opening comments made by a salesperson are critical to the outcome of the telephone call. The first few seconds will determine if their call will be looked upon favorably. Just as in a speech or a one-on-one visit, the salesperson must establish rapport. The immediate reaction to a telephone call is rarely neutral. This is particularly true when you are dealing with busy people. The role of the salesperson must be seen as "helpful" as opposed to that of a "pest".

Like giving a speech, be relaxed. Introduce yourself and the purpose of your call. Be brief and take frequent pauses to allow the customer to provide input. Always have some information that you wish to share and one or two questions for the customer. Speak with authority. Know what you want to say. Above all, be prepared to listen. If you are totally rejected, attempt to understand why. Focus on the customers needs, not yours. In the project business you should normally not be trying to sell on the telephone. Most calls are used to develop a stronger relationship with the customer.

At the end of the conversation, always establish a reason for getting back to the customer. This could include a follow-up call, an actual sales call or sending them something in the mail. This reason should be established prior to making the call. If a better reason comes up during the conversation, drop the original reason and use it. It is always best if the customer provides the reason. If they don't, invent one.

Written Communications

Of the five vehicles for communication, only writing offers documentation of that which has been agreed upon. Written communications play a more significant role in project selling than in any other type of sales because of the large amount of dollars involved. The consequences of a misunderstanding can be devastating to both the customers and the suppliers organization.

Written communications are also required within the salespersons organization to ensure the orderly pursuit of a project and to make certain that the key players understand what the company must do if an order is received. The good salesperson leaves tracks. Written communications is also used for interfacing with peers, buying influences, requests for information, thank you notes, etc.

Some Project Salespeople are Not Good Writers

Based on my experiences, a salesperson can probably be successful at project selling without being highly skilled in written communications. I've seen some very successful salespeople struggle by in this area. Unfortunate for them, they are missing out on a valuable tool that would round out their total communications skills. They get by in this area by using whatever skills they do have effectively. They must be especially strong in other communictions skills to offset their limitations in written skills.

Once the Decision is Made to Write - Do It

Most individuals are "well meaning" with good intentions to write a letter, note, memo, etc. but lack in follow-through. If a decision is made to write something on a given day, the probability that it will actually be done is greater than 50/50. If it is put off for one day, the probability drops to less than 50 percent. After the second day, it drops to 30/70 against ever being done, and each day thereafter drops exponentially. Written communications almost always has greatest value when it is done in a timely manner.

Writing Letters and Memos

In that written communications provides a "hard copy" on which our thoughts or ability to write might be judged, many people struggle with this form of communications. They become so involved with trying to choose exactly the right words that they forget about the message they are trying to convey. Written communications are often better if the individual just says what they want to say and doesn't worry about how their writing skills will be judged. One might get an "A" for letter writing and an "F" for accomplishing their purpose.

There is also a tendency by many to make every letter a work of art. I can relate to this because I sometimes get caught up in the same trap. If the consequences of the letter or memo are significant, certainly spend the time to get it exactly the way you want it. I find that my important letters are more organized and communicate my thoughts better if I prepare a draft of the letter in outline form prior to writing the actual letter. This may only take several minutes and will save a great deal of time when writing the actual letter.

Concentrate on the two or three items of most importance and attempt to keep the document short. One page letters and memos are great, two pages are okay sometimes, and three or more pages are boring and usually not read. If the document has to be longer than two pages, provide a summary of the contents at the beginning of the letter or memo.

Having Something Worth Saying

Writing a letter is somewhat like writing a check on your banking account. If you have enough money in the bank to cover the check, writing it is relatively easy. In the case of the letter, writing it should be relatively easy if you have something worth saying. If you have little to say, like the overdraft check at the bank, it will bounce and not be worth the paper its written on. Some of the rules that I follow when writing letters or memos are:

- What are the key points that I want to make?
- What response do I want from the reader?
- Is my message new to the reader?
- How informed is the reader on the subject?
- From ''one to ten'' how important is the letter?
- Will there be additional communication on the subject?
- Is a letter the best method to communicate my thoughts?
- Who should get copies of the letter or memo?

As with the other forms of communications, there are many books available on writing skills and during the past several months I have seen a number of seminars offered on the subject in most of the major U.S. cities.

Sending "Recognition" Notes

An easy and effective method of cultivating and maintaining quality relationships is the use of handwritten notes to communicate a feeling or thought. ''Thank you'' and ''Congratulations'' are examples of some of the more common types of personal notes. People like to be recognized for having done something special. Notes make people feel appreciated and important.

I strongly recommend that the project salesperson purchase one hundred blank notes along with envelopes. Purchase a like amount of postage stamps and place them on the envelopes. Everytime something of significance happens to someone you know, send them a little note sharing your feelings about the event. You will be absolutely amazed at how your relationships will strengthen. If you are sharing sincere feelings, you can't go wrong.

Reading for Business and Pleasure

To be effective, the salesperson must stay abreast with what is taking place within their company and with industry trends and new technology. To be successful, the project salesperson must be informed. One of the best ways that I know to stay current on events is to read.

A surprising amount of time with customers and fellow employees is spent on what I call "small talk". Customers like to buy from interesting and informed individuals. Reading about current events is one of the best methods of staying informed. It provides the reader with the time to study and analyze their feelings about issues. Written information also provides greater details than other medias offer.

As a project salesperson, subscribe to trade and industry magazines. If you want to be an expert in a field, any field, you have to be informed with the most recent information. Some of the best times for reading is what I refer to as "fill-in-time". Examples are; when on an airplane, train, waiting for an appointment, in the evenings when traveling, etc.

Well read people are more interesting people. Some reading should be done for pleasure. Select subjects that you enjoy. Spend time each day reading newspapers, magazines and books. On almost a daily basis my wife and I find a news item or article that we know the other would enjoy. By being on the lookout for each other as well as ourselves, we double the screening of published information.

Using Body Language in Selling

Although we have referred to using body language as a means of communications a number of times in these two chapters, I did want to share a few additional thoughts. Most of the discussions to this point have related to use of the eyes and eyebrows to both send and receive messages.

Reading body language is not as difficult as one might think. We all send messages through our bodies when we are: bored, angry, excited, interested, annoyed, friendly, unfriendly, impatient, tired, aloof, attentive, distracted, etc. The salesperson can often determine where they stand with a customer without a word being spoken. I once read that the human body has over 400,000 different non-verbal signs which indicates how an individual is responding to a thought. I've never taken time to count them but I suspect that there are more body signals than there are words in our language.

In addition to reading body signals, we send them. Our grooming and manner of dress send signals to those we deal with. Appropriate and new looking attire is the name of the game in selling. The salesperson should probably not wear a three piece suit when attempting to sell an irrigation system to a cattle rancher. The salesperson should dress for their surroundings. They should be neither "overdressed" nor "underdressed".

When interfacing with a customer, look interested and excited about the prospects of doing business with them. Listen to what they are saying with their words and their bodies, and respond with your verbal and body messages. It is somewhat like being in a stage play, although there may be many actors on the stage, only one speaks at a time. The others respond with body language.

There are several good books on the subject of body language, one of which is entitled . . . "Body Language" by Julius Fast. Most body language skills are learned through experience once the salesperson understands its importance.

In Summary

The development and use of communications skills is the enjoyable part of selling. In the project business, it isn't just important, it's everything. Products and services of competing organizations are often very nearly the same. It is the people selling the product that will make the difference between who will win or lose the sale. People buy from people.

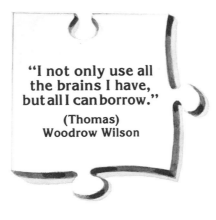

"I not only use all
the brains I have,
but all I can borrow."

(Thomas)
Woodrow Wilson

CHAPTER TEN

If Ya Wanna Win the Game...
Ya Gotta Field a Team

Most project salespeople spend more time developing their own
sales support team than they do working on their managers team.
To some extent, they are viewed as "loners" at sales meetings and
conventions. Although they have good working relationships within
the sales organization, their focus is developing relationships that
will help to close projects. The teams that they form do not show
up on organizational charts, nor are they visible to most people in
the organization. The team members, each an expert in their own
areas, are like the spokes of a wheel with the salesperson serving
as the hub to bring their talents together.

Although all types of sales require some form of team support,
the project salesperson is the most heavily dependent on the contributions and support furnished by other individuals. Not recognizing
the need for the development of this "personal support group" is
one of the major factors that keeps average salespeople from joining
the ranks of the Gunfighter. The inability to build the team, or
selecting the wrong team members, significantly reduces the probability for consumating an order on a targeted project.

Those individuals selected by the project salesperson as "team
members" have no direct reporting responsibility to the salesperson.
To infer that they even have a "dotted line" accountability to the
salesperson would raise concerns with most of their managers. On

many occasions, giving support to the salesperson actually takes them away from other assigned duties. I'm often amazed and in awe of the project salesperson that is able to get a disproportional amount of support and resources allocated to them and their projects. This is one of the primary reasons why a strong project salesperson must be managed by someone that understands the project business and the makeup of the Gunfighter.

The same disciplines and skills that allow the project salesperson to deal successfully with all types of customers are used to develop effective inter-personal relationships with other company employees and individuals that can assist them in their sales efforts. Being able to establish reciprocal support relationships with the analytical engineer, the amiable personnel manager and the extroverted sales manager are all in a days work for the project salesperson. They support him or her, not because of their job assignments, but out of a loyalty to the salesperson and because they believe that helping the salesperson to consumate an order is in the best interests of the company.

The "Quarterback" of the Team

I liken the project salesperson to that of a quarterback on a professional football team. They're not the coach, the manager or the owner of the team. Although they may call and execute the plays relating to projects, they don't decide how the business will be run and have little or no voice in the hiring of the other team players. Their job is to do the best they can with the team that is fielded. They must analyze the strengths and weaknesses of the opposing team and call their plays accordingly.

Maintaining Relationships from a Distance

In many situations, the project salesperson works in a geographic area that is remote to the home office. The skilled salesperson learns how to use this distance to their advantage and develops patterns of communications with key team members for maintaining on-going relationships. This constant cultivation of relationships during periods of time when the salesperson is expecting little or nothing of their fellow employees, keeps the door open for times when support will be requested.

Although there are many "tricks" to be learned in maintaining these on-going relationships, the major point that I wish to make is that the project salesperson recognizes the need to cultivate the relationships as a key ingredient to their success. It is the support given by others at critical times in a projects life that allows them to be consistent "winners" at selling.

One such "trick" is to learn the personal or professional interests of the team members. When the salesperson finds a newspaper or magazine article relating to that subject they send it to the fellow team member along with a short personal hand-written note. For the past ten years I have had the opportunity to work with a strong project salesperson that lives in Texas. Although we live 1200 miles apart, over the years he has sent me hundreds of clippings of articles that relate to my areas of interest. He enjoys sending them, I enjoy receiving them. Each receipt of an article helps to keep our relationship current.

Working With People at All Levels

An old sage of a salesperson once told me that the mark of a good salesperson is . . . "they are able to work with people at all levels of an organization". This ability to work effectively with all types of individuals, from the heads of organizations to the "common folk" allows them to be successful not only with their customers, but also with their fellow employees.

They use, but don't abuse relationships. They are constantly laying the groundwork for support and favorable decisions on strategic issues that may help them to close a major project or penetrate a new account. They may not always be successful in their efforts to get support on their projects, but they will always be given an audience with the decision makers.

Everyone Has Motives for What They Do or Don't Do

Salespeople are viewed as a unique breed by their fellow employees. Those employees that see themselves as "tied to their desk", envy the freedom of the salesperson. Others that believe they are "underpaid", may resent the commission or bonuses paid to the salesperson. When the salesperson purchases a new company car, some employees may view the money as coming directly from their profit sharing fund. Salespeople usually dress nice and have a great deal of self-confidence. Others in the company may view this as arrogance.

A number of years ago, while meeting with a data processing manager, I noticed a somewhat negative attitude on the part of the manager towards the sales organization. After several questions, I learned that he had a brother-in-law who he felt abused his privileges as a salesperson and was "ripping off his company". Based on this single instance he concluded that all salespeople took advantage of their companies.

I in no way wish to leave the impression that I feel that all other employees view the salesperson in a negative light. My point is that a significant number of people have a "misconception" of salespeople and it is in this environment that the salesperson works. In some types of sales, the salesperson may have a "who cares" attitude. For the project salesperson that is dependent on their team for support, they must understand the motives for their employees either supporting or not supporting their sales efforts.

Most employees would not provide assistance to the salesperson if they believed that the primary motivation of the salesperson was to earn a large commission or bonus. In fact, they will probably resent it. People are motivated to help others when they believe that the other individual is interested in their personal welfare and the well being of the company. In truth, successful project salespeople don't work for the money, they work for the challenge associated with accomplishing difficult tasks. The money is secondary and they show that in their behavior and their dealings with other employees. They never talk about the money they earned or lost on a project.

Selecting Team Members

During the remainder of this chapter we will discuss the types of individuals or positions within the company that the salesperson should target as members of their team. When a salesperson selects someone to be on their sales team, they must "sell" the individual on the benefits of team participation. It is usually not a direct conversation on the subject, but it evolves from the development of a relationship of trust. The answer to the question . . . "how do you motivate a thousand people?" is . . . "one at a time". Such is the way that team members have to be added. They are cultivated—one at at time.

Figure 1. provides a partial list of individuals that the project salesperson may elect to have on their sales teams. Team members will vary, depending on the product, industry and type of projects being pursued.

Figure 1.

Prospective "Project Sales" Team Members

- District, Regional and National Sales Managers
- Top Management (President, VP of Sales, Board Members, etc.)
- Engineering Personnel (Project Engineers, Department Head, etc.)
- Financial Personnel (Cost Accountants, Department Head, etc.)
- Customer Service and Contract Administration Personnel
- Manufacturing Personnel (Department Head, Production Manager)
- Shipping and Traffic Department Personnel
- Installation and Service Organization Personnel
- Company Secretaries, Receptionist, etc.
- Past and Present Customers
- Outside Buying Influences (Consultants, Industry Leaders, etc.)
- Networking Affiliates
- Spouse or Significant Other

Everybody Has a Boss

Most project salespeople report to a sales manager. Most sales managers have come through the ranks and have served as salespeople. Often the more successful project salespeople prefer not to become sales managers because of the administrative chores and because they are happy and are well rewarded financially. Therefore, a vast majority of sales managers come from the ranks of the Farmer salespeople. By their very nature they are service oriented and are inclined to focus on maintaining and growing existing accounts rather than charting new ground and exploring new opportunities.

The ideal reporting situation for the project salesperson is to report to a sales manager that has been a successful project salesperson. They talk the same language and think the same type of thoughts.

Early in the book we discussed the need for the project salesperson to have a mentor early in their career. When two project salespeople have the opportunity to work together as a team, both of them have a chance to grow and develop their skills even further.

The sales manager knows how much rope to give the salesperson and the salesperson knows how much rope to take before he or she will get into trouble with the manager. The project sales manager provides encouragement and support for the salesperson to establish their own support team and is not threatened by these activities.

One of the greatest frustrations for the project salesperson is to have to work for a sales manager that does not understand the project business. A Gunfighter cannot be managed like other salespeople. A ''good'' project salesperson will find ways to ''go-around'' a manager that doesn't understand the project business. This often frustrates the sales manager but they will accept the situation if the sales results are good. Project salespeople are also often negligent at submitting paperwork which can frustrate the sales manager.

The Gunfighter will decide early on in the relationship if the sales manager will be on their sales team. Most of them have the finesse to survive if they elect not to have the manager on the team. The single factor for selecting team members is whether their involvement will increase the probability for closing orders. If the answer is . . . no, they will not be a member of the team. In most cases the sales manager doesn't know that they have been excluded from the salespersons team, but they know that something is not quite right in the relationship.

Selecting the Offensive Line

The team members that directly support the project salesperson are like the offensive line to the quarterback. They protect his or her flanks. Although titles may vary between organizations, there is usually a customer service representative or a contract administrator that handles the details and paperwork of a proposal and also coordinates the contract once an order is received. This is the salespersons partner and their internal ''eyes and ears''. The bigger the project, the more details there are to be resolved and documented. They co-ordinate the contract terms, warranty, after the sale support, add-on pricing, payment terms, delivery schedules, etc. They are a key element to the success of the salesperson.

In project selling, meeting the specifications of a customers requirements are fundamental to obtaining orders and performing on contracts. The salesperson enlists the support of the engineering department for the technical support required to consumate orders. In some cases the product may have to be designed to meet the customers requirements. When calling for the support of other departments, the salesperson never relinquishes their responsibility for the overall management of the project. They monitor and approve all communications with the prospective customer.

Other departments frequently involved in the support of major sales are: accounting, manufacturing, shipping, installation, service, etc. Each project sale is unique unto itself and the salesperson must determine which departments should be involved in the sales pursuit.

You Don't Have to be a "Big Wheel" to be on the Team

The receptionist, the switchboard operator, the mail clerk, the sales secretary and many others are all part of the salespersons' team. The Gunfighter treats them with respect and courtesy because they know these individuals can play a contributing role in their success. They also establish these relationships because they genuinely enjoy interfacing with other company employees. In that they often operate remotely, salespeople tend to not take these individuals for granted as might the office personnel. The attention they give is highly appreciated.

The box of candy for the office staff at Christmas, the thank-you note for a special favor, the memo of commendation for a job well done on the switchboard, the friendly smile while visiting the home office are all methods used by the salesperson to re-inforce these relationships. The salesperson that takes these support people for granted will never know the joys they have missed or the support they may have lost at a critical point in the pursuit of a major project. The project salesperson builds a team of people that are looking out for their best interests. It is a natural "people" process. One good turn deserves another.

Dealing with the Company Brass

The bigger the deals, the greater the involvement of top management. If the salesperson is selling a standard product in small quantities, they will have little or no interface with top management. The project salesperson is a "wave maker" by pursuing the non-standard product or large volumes of business that have wide ranging implications on the organization. Many of these projects can and will reflect on the performance of the top management of the company.

In dealing in this environment, the salesperson must be competent. Projects should be researched and documented thoroughly. The salesperson that is trying to "sneak one by" is placing their company and themselves in a high risk situation. When called in by top management to defend or support a project, the salesperson should always be prepared and truthful. The salesperson should provide the decision makers with all of the known facts that will help them to make an informed decision. When dealing with projects, upper management wants to know that there will be ... "no surprises".

When interfacing with top management, relax and treat them with the same courtesy and respect that you would any other employee. However, always be in control of your enthusiasm, frustrations, anger, fear, impatience, disappointment, etc. Managers would prefer to base their decisions on available facts rather than emotions. Management appreciates employees with feet planted firmly in reality. Outward displays of emotion cause most managers to question the objectivity of the individual.

The project salesperson learns how to "weave" management into their projects as willing participants. The salesperson is competing for corporate resources. The more "winning" projects brought to the company - the greater the credibility of the salesperson - the more resources they will get for their projects.

Having a Customer Sell a Customer

One of the most effective team members utilized by the project salesperson is existing customers. Needless to say, it takes a very special relationship between the customer and the salesperson in order for the customer to play an active role in making a sale. Their involvement is usually limited to making a recommendation based on the past performance of the company. When used effectively, it can be one of the most powerful tools of the salesperson.

When there is mutual respect between the customer and the salesperson, the customer may actually appreciate being asked to make an endorsement of their product. In selling environments where there are a limited number of suppliers in a segmented market, customers may openly align themselves with specific manufacturers. I've often thought that this support is offered as a form of confirming that their choice of a supplier was the correct decision. To not support the supplier would mean that they had made the wrong choice.

The project salesperson knows which customers to select or avoid for endorsement of their product. The customer team member should be well informed about any project in which they participate. They should not be exposed to an unprofessional approach to selling.

Husband, Wife or Significant Other

Although my experience has been limited to my first and only spouse, most project salespeople that I have known have developed a relationship with their chosen partner who serves as their "sounding board" on all matters, including business. The "sounding board" is someone with whom they have an intimate relationship and knows them better than anyone else on earth. Single people can be effective at project selling, but those that have sounding boards have a distinct advantage.

Most spouses can cut through the "bull" and focus on the real issues that the salesperson is dealing with. They know when their mate is "up", "down", and when they are frustrated, impatient, tired and over-worked. Project salespeople operate on the fringe of being "workaholics" and when they are in the pursuit of a project they have difficulties in maintaining an "eight-to-five" workday. My experience has been that they select highly objective, "no nonsense" people as mates. Spouses have to be special people to live with the likes of the project salesperson. They are an important member of "the team". They help the salesperson to deal with reality.

Building the Team

The salesperson that tries to "conquer the world" by themselves will lose out to the competitor that utilizes all of the resources available to them. To be a success in the project business, one must learn how to be effective at "team selling".

"The sure way
to miss success
is to miss the
opportunity."
Philaretc Chasles

CHAPTER ELEVEN

Sales Prospecting -
"There's Gold in Them Thar Hills"

The opportunities for making sales are unlimited. Just as the gold prospector of yesterday had to decide which hills or streams to dig or pan for gold, so must the project salesperson focus on which sales opportunities to pursue. Once a salesperson has chosen a company and a product offering, they must then select the geographic territory in which they will pursue sales. This must be agreed upon by them and their company. A sales territory may be as large as the world or as concentrated as several blocks in a major metropolitan area. The size of the territory should be directly proportional to the level of opportunity the area represents for the companys' products.

Obtaining leads which represent potential orders is referred to as "sales prospecting". A systematic approach to obtain, qualify and pursue leads is absolutely vital to the success of the project salesperson. Unfortunately, the leads with the greatest potential often do not "stand out" from all the others and must be further qualified early in the sales pursuit process. In order to be effective at accomplishing this "qualification", the salesperson must establish a frame of reference to evaluate and prioritize all leads. The criteria used to prioritize leads can vary significantly, depending on the type of product and industry in which the salesperson works.

A "One Eyed Dog" in a Meat Market

Many salespeople view their sales opportunities like a "one eyed dog" in a meat market. There are so many "choice" opportunities to consider, they just can't decide where to focus their attention. Identifying and qualifying leads is a discipline that must be learned through experience. It is as fundamental to their success as their ability to close a sale.

Geographic Indexing

The collection and analysis of data relating to the number of prospective customers within a territory is referred to as "geographic indexing". The first step in this process is to divide the territory into geographical units (i.e. - countries, states, counties, cities, neighborhoods, blocks, etc.). These boundaries establish the "territorial rights" of the salesperson. It is within these boundaries that the salesperson should target their customer analysis.

In the opening moments of the movie, "Music Man", Robert Preston sang the song, "You Gotta Know the Territory", to the increasing rhythm of the turning wheels of the train in which he was riding. In the song he emphasized the need for the traveling salesperson to know everything taking place in their territory. This is also true of todays salespeople . . . "They Gotta Know the Territory".

There could be as few as twenty or as many as twenty thousand customers in a sales territory. In both cases it is essential that the salesperson know their customer base . . . how many exist and where are they located? As the number of prospective customers increases, the level of information about each will diminish. Geographic indexing begins by asking the question . . . "who has a need for my product?". If the number of prospective customers is so large that it is unmanageable, the salesperson may have to segment the opportunities into several target areas at which they will focus their attention.

The segments of a market that are to be targeted should be in harmony with the mission statement and intended direction of the company for which the salesperson is employed. Any inconsistency between the focus of the company and the salesperson is certain to result in disappointment and frustration for the salesperson, the company and most importantly, for the prospective customer.

As an example of geographic indexing, imagine that a salesperson has the responsibility for selling $75,000 x-ray machines in a three state area. The process begins with the question . . . "who has a need for my product?" In this example, the salesperson might start with identifying all the hospitals, clinics, doctors offices and industrial users of x-ray equipment in the three state area. If the number of prospective customers is large, the salesperson will have to decide how they would like to collect and arrange the customer information. One approach would be to place prospective customers into the four major categories mentioned above.

The major categories would then be sub-divided into additional groupings based on factors such as: size, number of patients, operating budgets, staffing levels, locations, services offered, existing facilities versus new construction, growth rates, trends, etc. This process of collecting information on the customer base is the first step towards the development of a sales "action plan". The x-ray salesperson in our example should determine if any of the customer information has previously been gathered. If not, it will be worth their time and efforts to develop the customer data base.

Where do You Get the Information?

Once a salesperson begins their search for information relating to their customer base, they will be amazed at how much relevant data can be collected, free of charge. The local library is a good source of information, as is the local Chamber of Commerce. Whenever I use a library, I first visit with the librarian and tell him/her the type of information I am searching for. They are almost always helpful and often enjoy working on special requests. If they do not have the information they can usually direct you to other sources. Many libraries have special business sections that are "ripe" with pertinent information relating to a broad range of industries.

Another excellent source of information often overlooked is to ask existing and prospective customers where you might gain information on their industry. I have found that they are usually flattered that you consider them an expert and are eager to help. When handled correctly, this process can strengthen your relationship with a customer. Every industry or market I am aware of has a professional trade group or society in which customer groups affiliate. With a little sales ingenuity, lists of the members of these organizations can be obtained. They are often available by state and city and also by their relative size and the specialty of their business.

Other sources of information on the customer base in a territory are: census data, county and state business reports, magazine articles, trade magazines, newspaper articles, competitors, the telephone book yellow pages, networking, etc. The most time consuming collection of customer information is what I refer to as "smokestack chasing". It is the counterpart to "cold call" selling and differs only by the fact the person is not necessarily trying to close a sale, they are only trying to identify a prospective customer. I recommend that this approach be used only when you have nothing better to do with your time or if the visit is highly convenient.

The Need for Good Leads

Early on in the book we identified the two types of professional commercial salespeople, the Farmer and the Gunfighter. Most of the Farmer type salespersons time is spent maximizing sales to existing accounts. Although new lead sources are important to the Farmer, their primary leads are their past customers. They concentrate their efforts on keeping the key decision makers at an account happy with their product, service levels and their individual support.

The project salesperson may do business with an account only once during their entire career. It is therefore essential that the salesperson have an ongoing source of new sales opportunities to pursue. The remainder of the chapter will deal with sources for these leads and how the salesperson can qualify, prioritize, and pursue these leads effectively.

Lead Generation and Follow-up

Although industries may vary somewhat, I have found that the vast majority of leads for all types of products and markets are generated through similar methods. In the case of a highly specialized product, the majority of the leads may come from a single source, but this situation would be relatively rare. Figure 1. provides a list of a number of common sources for generating leads. As you will note, the list has been divided into those methods used by the salesperson for generating leads, and those used by an in-house marketing staff.

Figure 1.

Common Sources for Leads

Leads Generated by Salesperson

- Referrals from existing customers
- Attendance at trade shows
- Networking with individuals with non-competitive companies
- Incoming telephone calls to salesperson
- Cold calling on accounts
- Trade magazines, newspapers, newsletters
- New construction reports
- Participation in customer related organizations
- Referrals by consultants, associates, etc.

Lead Sources Generated by Home Office

- Direct mail promotions
- Magazine space advertisements
  - Telephone response requested
  - Coupon response requested
  - Bingo card response requested
- Incoming telephone calls to home office
- Referrals from customers in other territories
- New product releases, public relations releases
- Personal acquaintances of company employees
- Conventions or exhibits not attended by salesperson

The responsibility for generating leads on a national or regional level usually rests with the home office product or marketing manager. The follow-up on these leads is assigned to the appropriate area salesperson. There seems to be an almost never ending difference in perspective on "lead management" between these two groups. The sales force complains the quality of the leads is inadequate and the in-house staff is disappointed in the "follow-up" by the field sales organization. There is often justification for these frustrations when the "hand-off" of the leads is poorly conceived and improperly executed. It is important for both groups to remember that they are a part of the same team and that in both cases their performance will be measured in terms of sales results.

The individual project salesperson has the ultimate responsibility for maintaining an adequate number of leads. They have the greatest vested interest in a specific territory and have a closer "pulse" for the activity level in their geographic area. I have always believed that it is the salespersons responsibility to place the necessary pressure on the home office staff for assistance in generating leads in their territory. It does little good to point fingers of accusation once sales results have fallen short of objectives. The salesperson must give specific direction to the home office as to what lead generating programs they would like to have initiated in their territory. They can anticipate a struggle for the use of company resources. They should stick to their guns and solicit other team members to support their cause. If successful, they will get a disproportionally high percentage of the companys' advertising and promotional budgets. In all companys, "the squeeky wheel gets the grease".

Some Types of Leads are Better Than Others

By their very nature, some types of leads are of a higher quality than others. The project salesperson learns to develop a "nose" for lead quality and always targets their efforts on those opportunities that they believe will yield the greatest sales results. The source of the lead is one of the key criteria used to determine its quality. During the past ten years I have been conducting an on-going evaluation of sales leads and the salespersons perspective as to the quality of various types of leads. Although the results of this study are from a relatively small sampling, the opinions have been highly consistent. The results of this evaluation are shown in Figure 2. The higher the quality of the source of a lead, as perceived by the salesperson, the higher it is on the comparison list. As you will note, I have assigned a weighted factor based on the inputs from the salespeople.

A number of observations can be drawn from the comparisons in Figure 2. One could conclude that a project salesperson would rather have one incoming telephone call from a prospective customer than to have ten leads that were generated from the use of a bingo card resulting from a product advertisement. Another example would be that they would prefer to have the incoming telephone call over four direct mail lead responses.

Figure 2.

Quality of Leads Evaluation

Rank	Lead Type	Description	Weighted Score
1.	Incoming Customer Telephone Call	Could be to home office or direct to salesperson.	1.0
2.	Outside Referrals	Consultant, architect, customer, etc.	2.3
3.	Qualified Convention Leads	Less than 5% of all convention leads. Funded projects.	2.8
4.	Inside Referrals	Through Direct interface or telephone contact.	3.0
5.	Direct Mail	Targeted to designated markets and users.	4.2
6.	Magazine Leads-Coupons	Customer fills in blanks and mails. They pay postage	6.2
7.	Trade Magazines	Listing of new projects for a specific industry.	6.7
8.	New Construction	Listing of new construction projects.	6.8
9.	Salesman Cold Call on Selected Accounts	In conjunction with other visits to geographic area.	7.3
10.	Unqualified Convention Leads	Only information is name & address plus info request.	7.7
11.	Magazine Leads-Bingo Cards	Reader circles your number on card in back. No postage.	9.7

All Leads Merit a Follow-up

If there is not a sincere intent to follow-up on leads, there should be no serious attempt to generate them. As we stated above, those responsible for generating leads usually do not have the responsibility for the follow-up. Although salespeople may form opinions as to the quality of a lead based on its source, it should in no way be inferred that some leads should be pursued while others are discarded. The single lead with the greatest potential may well be the bingo card that was returned by a prospective customer that is early in their decision making process. They may not be ready to select a final supplier to fill their requirements, but they could be collecting information to determine the three or four vendors from which they will make their final selection. This process is used by many companies.

Lead follow-up should be a joint effort between the "in-house" team and the "out-house" team. Together they form a single team. If we agree that all leads should be responded to in some manner, then the next step is to decide who will be responsible for each phase of the follow-up. If a product or market manager believes that they can pass on 150 bingo cards to a field project salesperson and expect that a phone call follow-up will be made to each of them, they are not living in the real world. Programs have to be designed to help move the quality of an individual lead to a higher bracket.

For example, lets assume that a company received 500 responses to a national magazine advertisement. A targeted direct mail program may then be the next step in the process of moving the lead to a higher quality. This step will place product information in the customers hands immediately and allows the "teaching process" of the customer to begin. If only three percent of the original respondents call a telephone number provided to them in the direct mail package, the company now has fifteen leads of the highest quality. If the prospective customer responds with a reply card included in the mailing, the quality of the lead has more than doubled.

The purpose of a follow-up direct mail program is to get a "second action" out of a prospective customer, which in effect moves them to a higher level on the quality of leads chart. Certainly the number of leads being generated will determine the follow-up process.

This is not to say that all of the leads should not be reviewed by the project salesperson. Many times a lead of any quality provides the reason to make contact with a new account of high potential or to develop a relationship with a key individual in an existing account. Also, the name of the individual or their position in a company may merit an immediate follow-up. Many times a lead can link you with an individual that is higher in the customers organization than a new vendor would normally interface.

Incoming Customer Telephone Calls

When a prospective customer calls expressing interest in your products, you've got a "live one". All employees that handle incoming telephone calls should be trained and instructed to deal with customers that are calling the company requesting information. These calls should be immediately turned over to someone in the sales organization. In the project business, the lead should be turned over to the salesperson on the same day, if possible, within the hour. The person that takes the call should not try to give too much information which might eliminate the purpose for the call-back by the project salesperson. This "first phase" of the mating dance can be very important.

Once the project salesperson has the request for information, the contact with the prospective customer should be made on the same day or at the very latest, the following day. I believe these calls to be of such importance, that my staff has standing instructions to pull me out of a meeting if necessary to take a call from a customer. A call from a prospective customer is more important than one from the president of your company. A customer will often measure the timeliness of your response as an indicator of how you will perform if you are given an order. Success in sales comes to those that make it easy for a customer to buy.

If you promise a prospective customer something over the phone, take the action immediately. Again, the salesperson will be judged on timeliness and follow-through. During the conversation and follow-up, identify some reason for making contact with them again in the immediate future. If nothing else, contact them to make sure that they received the requested information. The salesperson should document these early discussions with a customer in an internal memo for future reference. Although you should be tactful, attempt to qualify the lead to whatever level possible. People that are calling for information are often working on projects with "short fuses". If this is the case, they usually are willing to share a great deal of information. Get as many facts as possible without being obnoxious. Most of all, be a helper. The project salesperson is a problem solver. Attempt to understand the prospective customers problem.

Responding to Outside Referrals

The referral of a prospective customer by someone outside of your organization should receive the same priority as a telephone call from a customer. You may learn of the referral through a letter, telephone call or by direct contact with the prospective customer. When dealing with referrals, someone has cared enough about you or your company to endorse or recommend your product or service to another individual. This is one of the highest forms of a compliment that can be given in the selling profession.

The best referrals come from satisfied customers. In the chapter on team selling, we will discuss how the salesperson includes their customers as a part of their selling team. The manner in which this type of a lead is handled has implications not only on the prospective sales opportunity, but also on your relationship with the individual offering the referral. If the salesperson "drops the ball" and does a poor job in pursuing the prospective customer, it reflects back on the judgement of the person that provided the referral. They place their professional judgement on the line when they recommended you and your company to a business associate.

Networking for Leads and Referrals

Project salespeople are especially good at "networking" with non-competitive organizations. A slang phrase for describing networking is . . . "you scratch my back and I'll scratch yours". In the project sales business there is often a pattern where unrelated products are purchased during the same time frame by a customer. A salesperson often forms relationships with the salespeople representing the other companies and they share information on new projects. This can be a very effective method for obtaining high quality leads.

Other sources for referrals can include: consultants, designers, specification writers, trade association staff members, vendors, friends, business associates, etc. Referrals are an important element of lead generation in the project business.

Thanking an Individual for a Referral

The best "thank you" that a salesperson can give for a referral is to perform well on the lead follow-up and on the project performance if it becomes an order. Contact should be made with the individual that provided the referral to thank them and to verify that contact has been made with the prospective customer. This will help to ensure that future referrals will continue to flow from the same source. Scratch - scratch.

Convention Leads

As you will note in Figure 2., convention leads show up in two categories on the quality scale. They include both qualified and unqualified leads. Qualified leads are those prospective customer contacts where detailed information on their requirements have been discussed and documented. Over the years I have come to believe that many individuals that attend trade conventions or exhibits mentally increase their job status or authority when they are away from their home base. Many have illusions of grandeur and are not really in a position to deliver on the promises made at conventions. The greatest challenge of performing booth duty at conventions is to be able to separate the "decision makers" from the "literature gatherers".

Some of the problems with qualifying convention leads also rests with company employees that "man the booth". In the project business, the booth should be staffed with individuals that understand the project business. When a company has the opportunity to interface with a real "decision maker", the interchange of information is critical. For this reason, many companies staff their booths or displays with their top people, including company presidents and upper management. In order to separate the "wheat" from the "chaff" during trade shows, those manning the booth must be able to "read people". Attention should be given to the title of the visitor and their knowledge of their requirements.

The follow-up on qualified leads should take place immediately following the trade show with a telephone call from the project salesperson to the individual. An attempt should be made to get an audience with the customer at their facility. As can be seen in Figure 2, salespeople have a great deal of respect for qualified convention leads.

Unqualified convention leads usually consist of the name, title, company and address of the individual that visited the booth or showroom. At major tradeshows, larger companies may generate

10,000 or more unqualified leads. Each of these contacts should receive a follow-up letter and appropriate information on the products that were displayed at the exhibit. This is an attempt to move the lead higher in the quality scale. The salesperson for each territory should review all of the leads to determine if any of them should receive special attention.

Handling Inside Referrals

Leads are sometimes furnished by other company employees through friendships, contacts through outside activities, interface on industry committees, etc. These leads may come from members of the board of directors, officers of the company or even the janitor. These referrals should be handled much like the outside referrals discussed above. Inside leads are often taken too lightly and poor follow-up results. When an officer or fellow employee provides the salesperson with the name of a prospective customer, contact should always be made with the customer.

In addition to the lead representing sales potential, the method in which it is handled may have internal political ramifications. A follow-up with your actions should always be provided to the individual that offered the lead. The action can often best be accomplished with a short handwritten note thanking them for their involvement and an assurance that the opportunity is being pursued. If the project results in an order, the salesperson should ensure that they"share the glory".

Working with Direct Mail Leads

Direct mail programs to generate leads can result in very large response levels. In recent years, direct mail programs have come to play a much more significant role as the first contact with a prospective customer. The advances, and the abuses, made in this area during the past five years have been incredible. It is one of the best "first steps" in getting an initial response out of a prospective customer. If the mailing is targeted correctly and the company receives a response, the salesperson will be the recipient of some "hot" leads.

In a company with good marketing and promotion programs, the salesperson may be inundated with direct mail and magazine leads. Count your blessings. Heavy response usually means that there is a lot of interest for your product or services within the territory. Again, all leads should be responded to for the purpose of moving them up on the quality scale. If you have leads that are being unanswered, you are missing sales opportunities.

The Greatest Lead Challenge — Magazine Leads

There are two major objectives for placing magazine advertisement for commercial products. They are to generate leads and to enhance the image of the product or the company. Individuals that read magazines respond to advertisements for a multitude of reasons. I've come to believe that many of them are lonely people and enjoy contact by the outside world. Many others have a sincere interest in the products being advertised. A company that advertises must have a plan to manage their leads and separate those that have a serious interest in their product offering. One more time, each lead should receive a response.

Another reason for advertising would be to determine the level of interest in a product or service. If a product is new or the company has just entered a new market, their advertising may be focused upon "testing the water". Under these conditions, they may aggressively pursue each lead as a form of marketing research or to gain a base for the new product or market.

New Construction Reporting Services

Many companies are actively involved with the construction of new facilities or the major renovation of existing facilities. For those that are heavily dependent on new construction, there are several reporting services that track projects in the various phases of construction. These services can be obtained for various types of industries and for specific geographic areas of the country.

Based on the results of our quality of leads chart, I expect that I will hear from several of the companies that offer these services. These companies offer a valuable source of information on new construction projects but they require a great deal of time to understand and utilize the information. If a company is totally dependent on the new construction or major renovation of facilities, the reporting services is probably a must. I have found the service to be meaningful if it is the primary source for obtaining leads. Larger companies can staff to organize and administrate the continuing flow of information on new construction projects.

If a project salesperson is to use these services, they will have to spend a great deal of time to familiarize themselves with, and be prepared to analyze, numerous reports every work day. In order for the services to be justified from an investment standpoint, the information in them must be monitored on a continuous basis.

"Knock, Knock, Wanna Buy a Duck?"

In commercial selling, cold calls are a thing of the past. With the cost of an average sales call in excess of $200, front end qualification of each call is a must. I refer to cold calls as . . . "knock, knock, wanna buy a duck?" calls. The project salesperson avoids these low probability sales efforts.

More and more buyers are refusing to visit with vendors that haven't made previous contact and established some level of rapport prior to the first visit. The professional buyer appreciates the salesperson that pre-qualifies the account and has determined if there is a possible fit between their product and the prospective customer.

Timing is Everything

If there are ten vendors pursuing the same project, the first three or four that deal with the customer have the greatest chance for success. The first vendors have the opportunity to develop relationships with the buying influences and establish the standards around which the specifications are developed.

Getting into a project late usually means that the company will have to meet a competitors product standards and performance. Certainly some projects are won by the late arrivals, but they are faced with a much tougher selling job and their profit margins on the project are usually smaller. They often will receive the order only if they are the low bidder. The preferred supplier often does not have to be the low bidder if it is perceived that their product offers a greater value.

The project salesperson takes the management of their lead base seriously. It is the lifeblood of their future sales. Every lead represents an opportunity.

"Don't be afraid of
opposition. Remember,
a kite rises against,
not with, the wind."

Hamilton Wright Mobie

CHAPTER TWELVE

The Competitive Edge -
Knowing Your Opponents

Buyers have choices! Although that statement may appear to be overly simplistic, an understanding of it ensures that a salesperson takes nothing for granted when they are pursuing a sale. The project salesperson moves a project through each of its phases, recognizing the "power of choice" that the customer maintains.

Even during the final phase of a purchase, the customer has options. They may choose from one of a number of suppliers, divide the order between several suppliers, select a substitute product, re-define the need and purchase a different product, delay the purchase or eliminate the requirement. The project salesperson constantly evaluates the alternatives of the buyer and provides information which will result in favorable decisions towards the purchase of their product.

In the project business, the selling cycle begins when the first salesperson identifies a need or problem within a prospective customers' organization. From that point in time, the "race is on" between prospective suppliers. Creating a "competitive environment" is a process used by a customer to ensure that they will be able to purchase the best product for the most favorable price.

The Competitive Environment of Project Sales

In many selling environments, the salesperson may have little visibility as to which competitors are pursuing the same sale. One of the characteristics of "project selling" is that the salesperson usually knows which competitors they will face on a project. For this reason, it is important that the project salesperson have an intimate knowledge of their competitors. Their challenge is to persuade the buyer that their product offers greater value over competitive products. This "persuasion" can only be accomplished through an awareness of the competitive products and a knowledge of the strengths and weaknesses of the competing organizations.

Who Should Conduct a Competitive Analysis?

Collecting and evaluating information on a competitor is a team effort. The responsibility usually rests with both the "in-house" market and product managers and the project salespeople. If a company faces a competitor in all of their geographic markets, the primary responsibility for competitive analysis should rest with the home office staff. This eliminates duplication of effort. The results should be made available to each salesperson. If a competitor is active in only one territory, the responsibility rests with the salesperson with assistance provided by the home office.

If competitive information is not made available from the home office, the salesperson must take the responsibility for obtaining it. The salesperson has the greatest "vested interest" in obtaining and using the information. Project salespeople often form a network with other salespeople in the company to share information on common competitors. This is an excellent source of information in that it is usually current and represents the most recent strategies employed by the competitor.

When to Conduct a Competitive Analysis

When dealing with a "head to head" competitor, there should be an on-going effort to obtain and analyze information on the company. The salesperson must have an in-depth knowledge of these organizations and the information should be in a constant state of up-dating. When an event takes place which brings a new competitor into a salespersons' selling arena, one of the first steps that should be taken is to conduct an analysis of all of the elements of their organization. I refer to this "point-in-time" study of a competitor as a "competitive audit". Examples of events that may require an audit of a new or prospective competitor are shown in Figure 1.

Figure 1.

When to Conduct a Competitive Audit

- When expanding to a new geographic area with new competitors

- When facing a competitor on a project for the first time

- When introducing new products resulting in new competitors

- When entering into new market segments

- When new products are introduced which compete with yours

- When planning short and long range strategies

- When acquisitions, mergers or divestures take place

- When a competitor has a strong foothold in a target account

- When major changes are taking place with a competitor

Which Competitors Should be Analyzed?

In most project business selling environments, there are usually two or three major competitors that the salesperson will face on a frequent basis. It is these companies that should be the primary target for analysis and understanding. Competitors with a high market share are usually prime candidates for study in that they tend to influence the greater number of specifications and establish the industry norms. If the salesperson is in a niche market, they will want to target those competitors that are focusing on the same type of opportunities.

In some selling environments there may be numerous competitors, but the sifting out process tends to bring a salesperson major competitors down to two or three companies. One company that I work with faces 174 other manufacturers whose products offer a similar "form, fit and function." Needless to say, it is nearly impossible to effectively track the activities of 174 competitors. Under these circumstances, additional responsibility falls on the salesperson to focus their attention on those competitors that are the most active in their territory.

The greater the chance that a salesperson will face a specific competitor in the marketplace, the greater the need for the development of a competitive analysis. Maintaining accurate and up-to-date files on current and anticipated competitors is another of the "slight edges" the gunfighter is looking for.

What Type of Information to Look For

The salesperson should be able to mentally paint a picture of how a competitor looks to the outside world. Any information that can be found on a competitor is relevant, particularly information relating to one of their major competitors. The more frequent a competitor is faced, the more extensive the competitive file should be.

Rather than spending an inordinate amount of time on this subject, I have summarized the type of information that should be gathered in what I call . . . "the twelve P's of competitive information". This list is shown in figure 2. Several of these areas are elaborated upon in the following discussion.

Figure 2.

Things to Know About Your Competitors

Product - Benefits/Features, Strengths/Weaknesses, Quality, etc.

Personnel - Knowledge & skill levels, personalities, experience, value judgements, selling skills, number, etc.

Price Point - How does their pricing compare? Does price vary? Under what conditions?

Performance - Do they have a history for living up to their commitments? Who are their customers?

Past - How long have they been in business? Are they profitable? What level of resources do they have?

Position - From a strategic market positioning standpoint, are they a: leader, follower, challenger or nicher?

Persistence - How determined are they? Will they fight to the bitter end?

Patterns - How do they operate? What strategies do they employ? Are they professional? Are they predictable?

Pitfalls - Where are they the most vulnerable? Where is their Achilles Heel? Do they have dis-satisfied customers?

Pluses - What are they especially good at? Where do they shine? What customers endorse them? What are their strengths?

Poker - Are they good poker players? Do they know when to "hold em or fold em"? Are they good strategists?

Power - How strong are they? What resources are available to them? Do they have "staying power"?

Knowing the Competitors Product

The more frequently you face a specific competitor in the marketplace, the more you should know about their product. In the event you have a primary competitor, you should know their product as well as you own. This knowledge will help you in your strategic positioning on a given project. Many times a buyer will ask you the advantages of buying your product over that of a competitor. When this occurs, you have a beautiful opportunity to show how your product can fill their requirements better than that of your competitor.

·The salesperson should maintain a product file on each competitor. They should include copies of their brochures, specifications and published price lists. I avoid searching for confidential or privileged information. Having copies of information that is available on the open market is fair game. Usually the information stated in brochures will be included in the sales pitch by your competitors salesperson. When I have specifications of the competitive product, I always compare them to the users requirements to determine if their is a "match".

Later in this chapter I will discuss forty ways to get information on a competitor, but I did want to say a few words on getting published information. The best way I know is to ask your competitor for it. Many professional salespeople trade non-confidential information with their peers in other organizations. A good place to accomplish this is at trade shows or exhibits. Another method is to respond to their ads in publications or trade journals. If you prefer your business remain anonymous, have the information sent to your home rather than your business address.

Knowing the Players on the Other Team

If people buy from people, then the salesperson needs to know the people on the competitive team. I find this study of competitors team members to be one of the fun parts of selling. I like to go up against good competitors. Taking a project away from a formidable foe makes the winning even sweeter.

In professional baseball, the major league pitchers spend a great deal of their time studying the batting styles of the opposing team. The "heavy hitter" batters study the delivery techniques of the pitchers they will be facing. The project salesperson uses a technique much like the professional baseball player. They study the strengths and weaknesses of the opposing team members and use the knowledge to their advantage.

Each of us has certain "patterns" or styles in our modes of operation. People are predictable. When we know our competitors as individuals, we can better predict their next actions. I also like to have competitors know me and my salespeople. I work on letting them know that we will be in a competitive fight until the very last inning. By allowing them to know me, I get to know them better. I want to know the color of their eyes, their interests, communication skill levels, value judgements, previous success levels, etc. I like to have the same information on their boss and their bosses boss.

The more exposure the salesperson has to the competition, the easier it will be to form judgements. One of the best sources is to observe them in the pursuit of projects. Of particular interest is to observe how they behave under pressure when they lose a large project. This is a good measure of the character of an individual.

A good competitor is also "sizing you up" during this process of obtaining information. When you are in direct interface, make sure that you are "getting" more than you are "giving". New product and new market efforts are always out of bounds in the discussions. Again, the salesperson should always be focusing on "open market" information. Often the salesperson will be able to "read between the lines" to determine disharmony or disenchantment within the competitive organization.

Understanding the Competitors' Pricing Strategy

As projects get larger, one might believe that the difference in prices submitted by competitors would become larger. This is usually not the case, particularily when looking at the difference in bids as a percentage of the total sale. I've seen million dollar orders won or lost by as little as one tenth of one percent difference in prices. The larger a project, the more predictable your competitors will become. This is not to say that there won't be surprises, but you can usually determine why competitors take certain actions.

As we have previously discussed, the value of a product is a combination between the price and the quality being offered. A buyer trades off the benefits against the cost of a product. When involved in a competitive bid, it is the project salespersons responsibility to determine who the competitors will be on the project and to estimate each of their bid prices. They must also establish if the award will be made on price alone, assuming all of the suppliers meet the base specifications.

The first step in conducting a competitive pricing analysis is to determine which competitors will bid on a project. One of the best methods that I know to determine your competitors is to ask the buyer which other suppliers they are considering. In over ninety percent of the projects in which I have been involved, the buyer has been willing to share the names of the competitors. If you ask the buyer for this information they will almost always provide it; if you don't ask, they will rarely share the information. The salesperson can also look for other competitive signs such as; the visitors sign-in book, catalogs on the customers shelves or desk, competitor travel schedules, etc.

There are a number of factors to consider when attempting to arrive at an estimate of a competitors price on a project. Published price lists are certainly a place to start. Of greater importance is the competitors bidding history on projects involving the same product with similar quantity and delivery dates. The biggest single factor to consider is the importance of the project to the competitor. Factors that can change the bidding practices of a competitor are:

- They are the preferred/specified supplier
- They are not the preferred supplier
- They have production capacity not being utilized
- They are attempting to gain or maintain market share
- They are attempting to keep you out of an account
- The project has add-on potential
- The competing project salesperson has oversold the project
- The terms of the sale are changes (warranty, service, etc.)

Being able to estimate the competitors bid price is also a fun part of being a project salesperson. It is one of the best yardsticks for measuring the knowledge that a salesperson has about their competitors.

Watching for Competitive Patterns

One of the most effective ways of selling is to find patterns of operation that result in sales and then continue to do them over and over again. Competitors will also find patterns that work, and keep doing it until it stops working. How a competitor has operated in the past will be a good indicator of how they will operate in the future. As the salesperson "competitor watches", they should attempt to place themselves in the competitors shoes and predict their next move based on their past performance. What are their priorities? When you start to see their patterns change, try to understand what is bringing about the change.

Sources for Competitive Information

There are literally hundreds of sources readily available for obtaining information on competitors. Much of the information that ends up in my files was obtained by chance, not search. If the salesperson decides to always be on the lookout for competitive information, they will be amazed at the amount of relevant data that can be collected.

A number of years ago, while pursuing my MBA degree, a Ms. Peggy Milford and myself wrote a joint paper on the conducting of competitive studies. During our preparation of the paper we identified what we believed to be the forty most common methods of obtaining competitive information. Our list is shown in figure 3. As you may note, all of the sources on the list are ethical and within the limits of the law.

Figure 3.

Forty Sources for Competitive Information

- Dun & Bradstreet Reports
- Company 10K Reports
- Published Annual Reports
- Quarterly Reports
- Published Literature
- Contacting Present Employees
- Contacting Past Employees
- Writing to Request Information
- Published Trade Articles
- Competitive Public Bid Records
- Through Mutual Contacts
- Contacting Common Suppliers
- Transportation Companies
- Visits to Their Facilities
- Through Common Customers
- Through Your Customers
- Societies/Organizations
- Local Council Meetings
- Common Buying Influences
- Rumors
- Published Advertising
- Patent Searches
- Information at Conventions
- Visits with Their Salespeople
- Competitors not Common to Either
- Published Papers
- Attending Seminars by Competitors
- Local Newspapers-News Articles
- Help Wanted Classified Ads
- Published Price Lists
- Catalogs
- Past Lawsuits
- Interface with Financial Sources
- Resource Libraries
- Hiring Past Employees
- Printing Houses
- New Product News Releases
- Stock Market Trading Activities
- Union Contracts (Public Information)
- Testing Laboratories

Are Shady Methods Justifiable?

I think not. First of all, they're not necessary. Open Market information is far more easily obtained and it is almost always verifiable. The problem in dealing with gray areas, is that once you take that first step over the line, you've made the decision to operate on the fringe of the unethical. Once you've crossed the line, you've erased the boundaries of professional behavior. You may have read recently about the two U.S. casket manufacturers involved in a lawsuit which began with an over zealous employee of one of the firms going through the garbage of the other firm searching for confidential information. The individual in question ended up working both sides of the fence for personal gain and everyone lost.

The professional project salesperson doesn't need to have an unfair advantage. Those that take a "win at any price" attitude always end up losing. During the salespersons career, they will occasionally find themselves in a position where they are offered privileged or confidential information on a competitor. The information should be refused in a tactful, but firm manner. If you are good at what you do, you don't need that type of information. In truth, using the information may be the single factor that costs the salesperson the project. It may cause them to lose their stride and alter their normal approach to pursuing a project.

Sharing Competitive Information with a Customer

The project salesperson is often faced with the request by a customer to share information on a competitor. Sharing this information is within the scope of competitive selling and should not be viewed as negative selling. It all depends on the approach of the salesperson. The professional salesperson should know their product, the competitors product and the customers need or problem well enough so that they can counsel the customer.

Whether or not to share information on a competitor is based almost totally on the ability to read the customer. If the salesperson believes that their role is to teach and the customer truly wants to learn, then they may be able to reveal information that may strengthen his or her position. I always give the customer the prerogative of accepting or rejecting information that I may have on a competitor. If you do share information, make sure that it is accurate and can be substantiated. It should always be public, not confidential information.

Another time to consider using competitive information is when the salesperson believes that they are about to lose an order and the customer is mis-informed on the offering of the competitor. In these situations, the buyer may be unwilling to listen to the salesperson, and if they do, they may be turned off by the tactics. The customer has to be sold on the idea of requesting the information. If the salesperson believes that they are losing the project anyway, they are not risking the loss of the project, but they may be jeopardizing any hopes of building a future relationship with the customer.

I have seen a number of projects "pulled-out-of-the-fire" by offering the name of a customer that was dissatisfied with the product of a competitor or their performance on a project. Again, the customer must be "pulling-on-the-rope" in order for this information to be useful. It is only useful if the buyer can be motivated to make the call. If this strategy is to be used, the salesperson should furnish the name of the business, the individual to contact and the telephone number. The salesperson should never use this tactic unless they know the previous customer and have their permission to give out their name.

It's a Competitive World

Always take your competition seriously. If you are in a market where there appears to be little competition, then you are operating in a market that is either very small or things are about to change. On several occasions in my career I was involved with companies which experienced modest competition and relatively flat revenue growth. As soon as the company was faced with "head-to-head" competition, the market began to grow and both companies experienced growth.

I believe that a company is only as good as its competitors. I compare it somewhat to the development of a boxing champion. At some point in each fighters' career, they will find that they have developed directly proportional to the strengths and abilities of the opponents they have faced. If you want to be a champion in any field, you have to be willing to climb into the ring with a champion.

In the selling game, we become better at what we do only when we face competent competitors. We tend to learn very little from our victories and much from our defeats. The project salesperson can tell you a great deal about . . . "the-one-that-got-away", and very little about the orders they successfully landed.

"They can conquer
who believe they
can."
John Dryden

CHAPTER THIRTEEN

Secrets for Successful Sales Calls -
High Noon

All activities related to the development of the salesperson are in preparation for making effective sales calls. In the project business, most sales are made through direct interface with the customer. The large dollar size of projects and the complexity of the sale usually requires the "face to face" interchange of information between the salesperson and the customer. The probability for success on a project is always greater if there has been visual contact with the prospective customer. Most project salespeople are more effective in person than they are when using written or telephone communications.

During the past ten years, significant advances have been made in the techniques of selling through telemarketing programs. Many companies were forced to incorporate telephone selling programs due to the escalating costs of a field sales call. In the project business, the telephone is used to qualify projects and to obtain and provide information during the periods of time between direct sales calls.

The Escalating Costs of a Sales Call

According to a survey by McGraw-Hill of 1,714 vice-presidents of sales and sales managers in industrial companies, the cost of an industrial sales call in 1985 averaged $229.70. These costs have been escalating during each of the past ten years at a rate greater than ten percent per year. A ball park estimate on the annual costs to have a salesperson in the field is $70,000 to $80,000 plus bonuses or extra-ordinary commissions. Some of the direct and allocated expenses required to support a salesperson are shown in figure 1.

Figure 1.

Cost Elements Related to a Field Salesperson

- The salary and benefits package of the salesperson
- Travel costs - automobile, airfare, hotel, food, etc.
- Overhead costs for allocated office space
- The costs for any direct support staff - secretary, etc.
- Telephone, postage, overnight express, etc.
- Business entertainment costs
- Training and development costs
- Allocated sales meeting costs
- Professional memberships and subscriptions
- Convention or meeting costs within the territory

Note: Not included in the above list is the non-allocated costs of sales management and any direct support costs by in-house personnel.

As the size of a companys' field sales force increases, the average cost of a sales call usually decreases. Smaller sales organizations are faced with greater traveling distances and allocated expenses are spread over fewer salespeople. As field sales expenses continue to escalate, it becomes of increasing importance to maximize the results from each sales call.

The Age Old Question - How Many Calls Per Day?

Obviously, one of the ways to decrease the average cost of sales calls is to make more calls per day. The number of calls that can be made per day is dependent on the type of sales and the number of prospective customers in a geographic area. I know of successful salespeople that make only one or two calls per day and others that make five or six.

In most types of project selling, I would say that the salesperson should be making at least three calls per day, four days per week. The fifth day is spent on planning and paperwork. Most sales managers would prefer a minimum of four or five sales calls per day. There is no magic number of sales calls that should be made per day or week.

One factor that appears to have some relevance to the number of calls made per day is the average order size for the salesperson. The higher the average order size, the fewer the number of calls made per day. The lower the average order size, the more calls made per day. If the salesperson works only on million dollar projects, he or she may make only four or five calls per week. The remainder of their time is spent in preparation for the calls and in moving projects through their phases. A charting of the "one-project-at-a-time" salespersons order bookings usually looks like a view of the Rocky Mountains.

Establishing Patterns of Success

Successful salespeople, like successful businesses, must establish methods of operation that bring about desired results. If a pattern of success is not established, the salesperson must approach every opportunity from ground zero. Patterns relating to sales calls include the selection of which calls to make, when to make them, what to accomplish during the call and follow-up activities after the call.

The patterns of success vary between industries and the type of products being sold. Having been a sales manager in a number of companies, I would prefer to be able to establish patterns of success for the entire sales force and then implement programs to ensure they are followed. In truth, I have learned that the successful project salespeople will establish their own patterns based on what works for them. As a sales manager, I attempt to help them identify and crystalize the patterns.

131

One Gunfighter that I work with has established a pattern of making successful sales calls which has resulted in an annual compounding of sales revenues exceeding 25% during each of the past four years. The secrets he shared with me for penetrating and keeping accounts are shown in figure 2.

Figure 2.

One Gunfighters' "Pattern" for Success

Step #1. - Identify and target a key account based on potential.

Step #2. - Get "foot in the door" - get order for small project.

Step #3. - Perform well on the project. "On time" and "right".

Step #4. - Once account is developed, don't always attempt to be low bidder. The best position is second or third. Sell "quality" at an affordable price.

Step #5. - Always satisfy the customer, even if it means a loss on the project. Live up to your commitments.

Step #6. - Through all steps, give the customer personal attention.

Step #7. - When necessary, do the impossible. Work nights and weekends if necessary.

Step #8. - Make sure that the customers employees "look good". Go out of your way to help them in their jobs.

Step #9. - Integrate yourself into the organization. Gain "unescorted" access to their facilities. Be trustworthy.

Step #10. - Never forget steps 1. through 9. "out-service" and "out perform" all other competitors.

One of the first areas that I consider when dealing with a salesperson or a company for the first time is to determine if they understand their patterns for success. If they are unable to articulate a pattern, any success they are enjoying will be shortlived. If they have not been successful, it is because they have not established a pattern.

The Importance of Understanding Probabilities

Making successful sales calls requires more than just "making a good sales pitch" to prospective customers. Of equal importance is to decide which customers should be targeted for a sales presentation. Project selling requires the right pitch, being presented to the right customer, at the right point in time. The successful salesperson must be able to identify the merits of each project and decide which projects should be pursued.

Those that are successful at project selling learn how to "rifle" their efforts at opportunities rather than using a "shotgun" approach to selecting targeted customers. In todays marketplace, being a good salesperson isn't enough. The salesperson must be able to "weed out" those projects that would be difficult to close, and focus on those that represent opportunity. Eliminating the wrong project is as important as selecting the right one.

During each phase of a project, the salesperson should ask themselves . . . "what are my chances for success on this project?" In order to be able to do this, they must establish some frame of reference to qualify the merits of each project. The most successful method that I know of to establish these "reference points" is to assign "probabilities of success". Each project is assigned a probability for success, based on the circumstances relating to the sales opportunity. These probabilities are used by the salesperson to establish their priorities as to which project to pursue and as a common "language" when discussing projects with fellow employees.

It is important that the salesperson and everyone on their sales team use similar guidelines when assigning probabilities. Figure 3. provides the guidelines that we established for a company I worked with in 1977. These guidelines are still being used today. Once the guidelines are established and agreed upon, everyone on the team understands the chances of getting an order. If the chances are poor, and the efforts to get the order are significant, the company may decide not to pursue the project.

Figure 3.

Assigning Probabilities to Projects	
(One company's guidelines)	

Probability	Criteria
5%	Used primarily for large projects that have a high degree of uncertainty. Little information available.
10-20%	The funding for the project is uncertain, few facts are available, specifications are uncertain, strong competitive activity is anticipated.
30%	The funding for the project is approved or is eminent, strong competitive environment.
40%	The project is funded, we are one of two or three suppliers being given serious consideration.
	Note: All probabilities greater than 50% are funded projects, regardless of the preference for our product and company.
50/50%	At this level, we have an equal chance of winning or losing the order. Usually only two suppliers being considered.
60%	We have received feedback that we are the preferred supplier. The order placement is greater than 30 days away. We have two ''champions'' on the project.
70-80%	We have current and extensive visibility into all buying influences. Our product is specified. Order will be placed within 30 days. Two or more champions support our product.
90%	Customer has given verbal confirmation that we are the selected vendor.
95%	Customer provides us with a verbal purchase order.
100%	We have the written purchase order in hand which authorizes us to procede with production and shipment.

Using Probabilities for Forecasting

In companies that are heavily dependent on project business, there is a direct forecasting relationship between the dollar size of projects, the probability of success for each project and the number of projects being pursued. This relationship can be used to forecast anticipated incoming order levels.

The estimated dollar value for each project is multiplied by the probability of success assigned to the project. The resulting dollar value for all of the projects are then added together to obtain an estimate of all anticipated orders. The company will be successful on some of the projects and others will be lost. If the probabilities were assigned correctly, the law of averages should work to bring the actual incoming sales relatively close to the forecasted levels.

Preparing for the Sales Call

In the project sales business, the salesperson never goes on a sales call without being thoroughly prepared. In some types of sales, the salesperson may be able to "wing it" on a sales call. When working on major projects or pursuing a key account, the stakes are too high to risk "taking chances".

As you already know, I don't believe in cold calls and believe that the salesperson should be working on qualified leads. A qualified lead represents a "real" opportunity. The salesperson should approach each call as if it were their only chance to meet the most important customer they will ever deal with. If a sales call isn't important, the salesperson shouldn't be wasting their time on the account.

Some of the factors that the salesperson may wish to consider during their preparation for a sales call are shown in figure 4. In reviewing the list, you may wonder how much of this information can be obtained prior to the first "face to face" with the customer. It has been my experience that a great deal of information can be obtained. The type of business that a customer is in can tell the salesperson a great deal about their product requirements. Also, a significant amount of information can be generated during the lead qualification process. The first sales call may be the last if the salesperson hasn't prepared diligently.

The estimated size of the opportunity will determine the level of preparation for the first sales call. Good preparation helps the salesperson ask the right questions during the visit.

Figure 4.

Factors to Consider When Preparing for a Sales Call

- What problem is the customer attempting to solve?
- Does my product solve the problem?
- What do I want to accomplish at the sales call?
- Have we sold to the customer before? How did it go?
- What is the best estimate on project dollar size?
- What do I know about the customer? What do I need to know?
- Have they previously purchased from a competitor? Who?
- Who am I dealing with? Do they have the authority to buy?
- Is there follow-on business to the original purchase?
- What is the timing of the project?
- Is the customer financially sound? Do they pay their bills?
- What information do I want to learn during the visit?
- Should any other "team members" be present during the call?
- Should I leave any information with the customer? What?
- What reasons will I give for making a "follow-up" to the call?

The Importance of the First Sales Call

If the salesperson is going to be "knocked out of the saddle" and eliminated from a project, it will usually happen on the first sales call. Many customers approach vendor selection much like the process of selecting a beauty queen. They narrow the field to two or three finalists from which they select the winner. The first visit with a customer is often the time when they select the finalists.

Making the first sales call is somewhat like asking someone to dance for the first time. If "magic" doesn't occur during the dance, the relationship will probably go no further. In the case of the sales call, if there isn't some rapport developed between the salesperson and the customer, the probability for success drops significantly.

The First Visit - A Time to Learn

In a previous chapter I stated that the salesperson should often view their role as a teacher and the customer as the student. In the first sales call, these roles are reversed. The salesperson can't determine that his or her product is right for the customer unless there is an understanding of the customers' requirements. The role of the salesperson is to ask relevant questions. The salesperson will be measured more on their level of interest in the customers problem than they will be on their selling ability.

To place myself in the proper "mind-set" for the first visit with a customer, I sometimes visualize myself as a giant sponge. My purpose is to soak up all of the information that the customer is willing to share. When I leave the customers facility, I am saturated with vital information. The sorting out of the information can be accomplished later when I can fit all of the pieces together like a giant puzzle.

In figure 5. I have listed a number of examples of questions that should be answered during the first visit. As you may note, some of the questions are duplicates of those shown in figure 4. relating to the preparation for a sales call. The first visit is the time to confirm or refute any information that may be known about the project. Most of the information that the salesperson wants is the same information that the customer wants to give them. The salesperson serves as a facilitator to get the customer to bring out the vital information.

Figure 5.

Questions to be Answered During the First Call

- What problem is the customer trying to solve?
- Is the project funded?
- Who is responsible for making the decision or co-ordinating the purchasing activity?
- What other individuals are involved in the decision? Can they be contacted?
- What is the size of the project? (Dollars, # of units, etc.)
- Is there presently a preferred supplier? If so, who?
- What is the timing of the project?
- Are there any outside buying influences? (i.e. - architects, designers, consultants, etc.)
- Have product specifications been developed? What are they?
- If the project has not been funded, what events have to take place to make funding available?
- What factors will be considered other than price? (i.e. - warranty, service, support, etc.)
- Are there any special requirements for the successful vendor? (i.e. - performance bonds, insurance, union labor, etc.)
- What are the terms for payment? (i.e. - front end payments, progress payments, hold-backs, etc.)
- Who are the competitors?
- What can the salesperson do to help the process?
- What reasons can be used for a follow-up to the call?

Establish a Reason for a "Follow-Up" Action

During all sales calls, especially the first, the salesperson should establish a reason for a follow-up contact with the customer. The salesperson should be sensitive to possible reasons for a follow-up during the course of the meeting. Select the very best reason possible. Often the reason is provided by the customer during the course of the conversation.

Don't state the reason for follow-up until the end of the meeting unless the customer asks for information that you do not have with you. On occasion I may have the requested information with me, but I may hold it in reserve as the reason for a follow-up call. A follow-up action may be a telephone call, something sent in the mail or a second visit. These timely actions are signals to the customer that the salesperson is "working" the account.

Being There at the Right Time

The project salesperson has a "nose" for being able to determine when the timing is right for the first sales call and/or the critical sales calls. If the visit with the customer is too early, the customer may not be mentally willing to listen and absorb what the salesperson is saying. They are not yet ready to begin the mating dance. When the time does come to make a purchasing decision, they may not contact the salesperson because they believe they have already heard the sales pitch.

If the sales call is too late, the customer may already have a preferred supplier. If the customer is still willing to meet with the salesperson, it is usually out of courtesy or an attempt to satisfy their superiors that they have evaluated all prospective suppliers.

One of the best ways to determine the timing of a sales call is to ask the customer for guidance. If the salesperson asks the right questions, the customer is usually willing to share pertinent information. The timing of sales calls is much more critical to the Gunfighter than it is to the Farmer. The Farmer develops on-going relationships with accounts, the Gunfighter works with accounts when major projects are taking place.

The Scheduling of Appointments

The manner in which a project salesperson "fills" their schedules is critical to their success. As a sales manager, I can usually tell if a salesperson is scheduling their activities far enough in advance. The salesperson should be planning around a thirty day "window of activity". If I make contact with them and request a meeting for a specific day the following week and they are able to oblige me, I know that they do not have meaningful activities planned for the week.

One of the ways to distinguish between the Farmer and the Gunfigher is to ask them their schedules for the next thirty days. The Farmer will tell you what cities they plan to visit. The Gunfighter will tell you which projects they will be actively pursuing. When pursuing projects, the schedule is driven by the phases of the projects. If a project is "coming down", that will be the major area of concentration for the salesperson.

Planning Time Gaps for "Extraordinary" Events

Imposters of Gunfighters will often tell their managers that they are leaving their schedules open so that they can respond quickly to unanticipated opportunities. The real Gunfighter fills their schedules as full as possible for at least a two week period. If a new opportunity comes to the surface or a key project moves faster than expected, they will adjust their schedules based on the merits of each opportunity.

The salesperson that does not plan their schedules well is somewhat like the individual guiding a snowball down a hill with a stick. As the snowball starts to get bigger, it becomes more difficult to control. If the salesperson does not manage their schedule effectively, the events that take place begin to manage them and become out of control.

The Development of Champions

In project selling there are usually a number of individuals in various departments that are involved with selecting a supplier. The salesperson that is first to convince any two of the decision makers that their product provides the best solution to the customers requirements has a significant advantage over other suppliers. I refer to these individuals with a customers organization as "champions".

The development of champions is an art unto itself. The salesperson learns how to avoid "stepping on toes" when working with the various departments in a customers' organization. To be successful at champion development, the salesperson should identify what each member of the selection committee believes to be important. The salesperson should understand the viewpoint each member will have in selecting a vendor. Figure 6. provides examples of prospective candidates for champion development.

Once two champions have been developed and they are willing to fight for the salespersons' product, they will look for ways to convince other members of the selection committee on the merits of the product. At that point, the salesperson should supply them with any requested information, and let the champions do the selling for them. The best champion is the one that controls the purse strings. Many of the committee members can say "no" to a specific supplier, but only a few of them, sometimes only one, can say "yes".

Figure 6.

Candidates for "Champion" Development
(Within the Customers Organization)
- The buyer handling the project
- The Purchasing Supervisor or Purchasing Agent
- The Project Engineer or Engineering Supervisor
- The Cost Analyst or Accounting Supervisor
- The Facility Manager
- The actual end-user of the product
- The Department Head of the end-user
- The President of the company or other interested officers
- Outside buying influences (Consultants, Architects, etc.)
- The Project Manager (if one is assigned)
- Any staff assistants, secretaries, fact finders, etc.
- Other individuals participating in the decision

Keeping the Ball in Your Court

At the conclusion of each sales call, the salesperson makes sure that the responsibility for the next contact rests with them. On occasion, the salesperson may ask the customer . . . "when would you like me to contact you again?". I never ask this question unless I already have another reason for a follow-up call or information I will be sending them. If the salesperson allows the customer the option of taking the next initiative, they may be setting themselves up for a long wait.

I often envision the relationship between the customer and the salesperson as two individuals on the opposite ends of a rope. If the salesperson advances the rope too fast, it all collects in a pile between the two of them. If the rope is advanced too slowly, the tension on the rope becomes too great and the customer becomes frustrated. The good salesperson knows how fast to feed the rope based on their ability to read the customers signals.

Documenting Sales Calls

Following each sales call, the salesperson should document, in writing, the discussions that took place at the meeting. Points that may seem insignificant at the time may be of major value as the project matures. Copies of the documentation should be sent to those individuals within the company that will be involved with the project, especially to team members that will play a role in the sale.

The notes will also help the project salesperson identify any changes that are taking place in the position of the customer. The best time to document the meeting is immediately following the sales call. Each salesperson should use methods most comfortable for them, but I have found that the use of a dictaphone documents the details of a meeting better than other methods. I use my notes from the meeting to ensure that I am covering all of the major points discussed.

Finding "Win-Win" Combinations Results in Sales

The ultimate decision to select a specific vendor is often based on a number of factors, but paramount to all selections is the overriding question by the customer . . . "in whom do I want to place my trust?". In business transactions there are four possible outcomes between two parties. They are:

I Win — You Lose

You Win — I Lose

You Lose — I Lose

You Win — I Win

Of the four possible outcomes for a business transaction, only the last is acceptable to the project salesperson. It is less a matter of ethics than it is a practical matter. If the customer believes the salesperson is only interested in getting the order, they will not place their trust in that individual. The good salesperson will walk away from an opportunity if they know that their product will not meet the customers requirements. In almost every case that I can remember, when I or one of my salesmen pulled back from a project and informed the customer that we could not meet their requirements we were rewarded twofold on later projects. If you are the customer, in whom do you wish to place your trust?

"To find a career to which you are adapted by nature, and then to work hard at it, is about as near to a formula for success and happiness as the world provides."

Mark Sullivan

CHAPTER FOURTEEN

Settling Down, Moving Up, or Moving On

The Gunfighter likes to "live on the edge". They thrive on challenge and if they become bored or underchallenged, they will make a career change. Many individuals who are unhappy with their jobs, stay in the position for years, afraid to make a change which might impact their financial stability. Most Gunfighters don't think this way.

When the Gunfighter does decide to make a job change, it is rarely because of money. They are among the 20% of the sales staff that make 80% of the sales and they are usually highly compensated. Also, they are less "money motivated" than they are "challenge oriented". This does not mean that money is not important, but it is a secondary issue.

The career options of the project salesperson are similar to those in other vocations. They can remain in their current position, move laterally to another position in the organization, be promoted or change companies. The lateral move is rarely an option for the project salesperson. In this chapter we will discuss the "pros" and "cons" of the remaining three alternatives.

Similarities Between Gunfighter and Entrepreneur

There appears to me to be a great deal in common between the Gunfighter salesperson and the entrepreneur. In fact, many entrepreneurs are Gunfighters and many Gunfighters are entrepreneurs. Both are highly challenge oriented, are willing to take risks and are comfortable in dealing with rejection. Another similarity is that many of them are poor people managers. They are often impatient and have very high expectations of themselves and everyone that works for them.

The major difference between them is that the entrepreneur is able to visualize opportunities and is willing to risk their net worth to pursue them. The Gunfighter also recognizes opportunities, but does not risk his or her own assets. Another difference is that the Gunfighter must develop their skills in order to be successful while the entrepreneur spends little time on self development activities. They are driven by instinct and intuition.

Individual Performer Versus People Manager

The success of the project salesperson is usually highly visible in an organization and they are recognized as individuals that make things happen. For this reason, they are often considered for promotion, usually for a sales management position. Although we will discuss this possibility later in the chapter, there is a fundamental issue that relates to any change made by the salesperson, and that is that they must decide whether they want to be an individual performer or manage other people.

As with most management positions, being a project sales manager requires a double skill level. First they have to have the aptitudes and skills of the project salesperson and they must have the ability to get results through other people. Many project salespeople have both of these abilities, others do not.

The importance of moving qualified Gunfighters into management positions is that they have an understanding of the project business and they will be able to accelerate the development of other project salespeople. If a company is highly dependent on project business, the continuing development of their sales force is an absolute must. Although training programs can be designed for the entire sales staff, the development of a salespersons' ''project selling skills'' must be handled on an individual basis between the manager and the prospective Gunfighter.

Some successful project salespeople are better "doers" than they are "leaders". Their skill levels come natural and it is often difficult for them to demonstrate to others what they do to be successful. They are "hands on" people and have trouble delegating responsibility to their subordinates. To some extent, they are like the aerobatic pilot of an airplane. Those that are the most skilled in flying a plane in stunt maneuvers may be the least able to teach a new student the fundamentals of flying. Their skills often come from "the seat of the pants". The student may be better served by learning from someone that also had to follow the steps carefully to learn how to fly.

Project Selling as a Life-Long Career

During the past ten years the stature and appreciation of the role of the professional salesperson has increased significantly. The key word in that statement is "professional". Being professional in sales is a combination of; consistent performance, ethical behavior, customer problem solving, product and industry knowledge, aggressiveness, etc. There is an obvious reason why the project salespeople in many companies receive compensation equivalent to the vice president of sales. The contribution of both positions are considered to be equivalent. A good project salesperson is worth their weight in gold. Well, almost.

If the project salesperson can find success, contentment and happiness in their lives, they should recognize their good fortune and continue with their chosen path. As I mentioned earlier in the book, all three of these conditions are individual attitudes. The salesperson that is contemplating a career change should spend time taking inventory of what they want out of life. The following definitions may help in placing these three states of mind in perspective:

- **Success** - I like myself and what I have accomplished.

- **Contentment** - I appreciate my life without having to compare it to other individuals.

- **Happiness** - Not necessarily living a dream fantasy, but liking what you do. Happiness is knowing who you are and being glad of it.

Several years ago I read a reporters' interview with Kenny Rogers, the entertainer and businessman. Mr. Rogers said that the best advice he had ever received was . . . "the most important thing is to think of yourself as a professional, and act that way. You must be willing to work at your craft, and be willing to face lots of disappointments. No one can do it for you. People ask me all the time to help them get started, but no one can make anyone else a success."

Each of us must decide for ourselves what is "right" for us in our careers, although we should be guided by those we trust. The project salespersons' career alternatives are somewhat unique in that it is one of the few vocations that I know of where the individual doesn't have to look at accepting a promotion as their only means to earning more money. In many other vocations, financial success is achieved only by "moving up the ladder" of the organization.

Using the Talents of the Project Salesperson

One of the best methods of keeping a project salesperson productive and satisfied with their current position is to assign them responsibilities other than their pursuit of projects. These duties should not interfere with their sales responsibilities, in fact they should compliment them.

Project salespeople often have strong egos. If they are ignored and have little input into establishing the direction of the company, they will become disenchanted and begin to question management decisions. By using their talents in areas other than direct selling, they feel closer to the organization and the company benefits by their contribution.

Figure 1. provides a list of some of the activities that could be assigned to a project salesperson. The sales manager should ensure that the salesperson does not have more than two or three added responsibilities so that they do not detract from their sales responsibility.

Figure 1.

Special Assignments for the Project Salesperson

- To serve as the company's representative to national associations
- To monitor and report on an assigned market segment
- To participate in regional trade associations
- To prepare reports in areas of their expertise
- To manage designated national accounts that may have their home office in the salespersons' territory
- To serve as the "eyes and ears" of competitive activity and to provide reports on the information
- To recognize and report on industry trends
- To make presentations at sales meetings or other company meetings
- To serve on committees that relate to their area of expertise
- To speak at trade shows or conventions
- To identify and report on new product or market opportunities
- To assist R & D efforts through their contacts with customers

---

The salesperson is in an excellent position to serve as the companys' "eyes and ears" on market and competitive activity. They are often the first company employee exposed to a new competitive product or to new opportunities which are appearing in the market. The company should establish policies and procedures which ensure that the salesperson is encouraged to submit information of this nature. The individual that receives the information at the home office should ensure that the salesperson is thanked for the information and is given feedback on how the information was used. Like all of us, salespeople need encouragement to participate in activities that fall outside of their normal responsibilities.

The project salesperson is also an excellent choice for making presentations at sales meetings or other company gatherings. Their verbal skills are strong and they often present a perspective which is "fresh" to the home office staff or their sales peers. Their presentations tend to be "straight to the heart" of an issue. They are also excellent candidates for representing the company at trade shows and conventions.

Motivations for Seeking Management Duties

If the project salesperson isn't motivated to accept a promotion for monetary reasons, then what factors do contribute to their decision? The reasons vary with the individual, but most often I have found that they accept the position because it represents a new challenge. Other reasons for accepting a promotion are shown in figure 2.

I view all of the reasons in figure 2. as being honorable motivations if the project salesperson believes in their heart that they are the most qualified and best suited individual to fill the position. In addition, they must be committed to being successful in the position.

Figure 2.

Reasons for Pursuing a Sales Management Position

- The desire for change and challenge

- To use as an entry level to upper management

- To avoid "working for" and "training" a new sales manager

- The desire to teach "project selling" skills

- Ego drive - title, status, success, etc.

- Enjoys competing for the position

- Wants to have a voice in the selection process

- Has a genuine desire to be in a leadership role

- Sees position as a way to "shape up" the company

- Inter-rivalry with other salespeople

- The fear of significant change with new sales management

Sometimes a person has to do what a person has to do. Most project salespeople, even those that do not have people management skills, will take a sales management position at least once in their careers. It is often a disaster for both them and the company The individual should always recognize what they are giving up to go to a new position.

What Does the Salesperson "Give-Up"

The most common promotions that a salesperson receives are to be named as a district, regional or national sales manager. Many project salespeople also qualify for product or market manager positions. a position that appears to be gaining acceptance in many companies is a national accounts manager which handles one customer that does business on a nationwide basis.

The salesperson sacrifices less if the new position operates out of a field office. Any promotion that requires that the salesperson move to the home office will probably take the greatest amount of adjustment. We will discuss this in a later paragraph.

By accepting any promotion, the salesperson gives up some of their freedom. The salesperson that operates independently in the field has a great deal of flexibility in managing their time. They must have a strong desire for the new position in order to give up this freedom.

The greatest sacrifice is for those salespeople that are paid "open ended" commissions. Although their base and benefits may be about the same in the new position, managers usually have "caps" on their compensation packages. Most management positions have a high base salary along with a bonus based on performance. It is relatively common for the base salary to represent 75% of their total compensation with a year end bonus making up the remaining 25%.

If the new position requires a move to the home office, the salesperson will often have to sacrifice the use of a company car. Prior to 1986, this was an important factor to the salesperson, but the new tax laws have reduced the benefits of driving a company car.

What Does a Sales Manager Do?

In order to be effective, the sales manager has to be proficient in five areas of management. If they are weak in one area, their total effectiveness will be greatly reduced. The five areas are:

151

- To hire (competent salespeople)
- To fire (incompetent salespeople)
- To train (all salespeople)
- To motivate (all salespeople)
- To make the numbers (sales objectives)

All five of the above duties of the sales manager require people skills. Having a successful track record as a salesperson and knowing a product and/or an industry are not enough to ensure success as a sales manager. As stated earlier, the sales manager must get results through people. There are many techniques and disciplines that can be learned to improve an individuals skills in the first four areas listed above.

Consistently making sales objectives requires a certain "frame of mind". Certainly it is highly dependent on getting the job done in the other four areas, but it is also a specialty unto itself. It begins with being realistic when establishing objectives, and is dependent on having a "can do" attitude in pursuing the objectives. Once the objective has been agreed upon, it is up to the sales manager to "make it happen". If obstacles arise, they are responsible for "knocking them over". Most sales managers were successful as salespeople in achieving their sales objectives. In their new position as manager, they must ensure that others achieve their objectives.

Culture Shock - Working at the Home Office

Most national sales managers, national accounts managers and product and market managers work out of the corporate offices. This ensures that there is frequent and accurate interchange of information between the sales management organization and other departments such as; marketing, manufacturing, engineering, finance, human relations, research, customer service and top company management.

If the project salesperson has had a great deal of freedom in the field, a move to the home office can come as quite a shock. Most of their schedule was the result of "self-imposed" duties and activities. The time spent in the new position will be consumed and driven by "system imposed" and "boss imposed" duties. The higher an individual goes in an organization, the greater the need for cross-communications to take place between departments.

Living in a World of Meetings

When the salesperson operated out of the field, one of their greatest frustrations was not being able to reach people because they were in meetings. Now they will be one of those that will be in the meetings, and they may not adjust well to this environment. Although the individual can work at minimizing meetings, the fact is that many of them are necessary and cannot be avoided. Many people fight meetings. Don't fight em, help to make them shorter. We discussed this subject in chapter nine which related to developing communications skills.

Adjusting to a "Routine" Schedule

Salespeople are accustomed to establishing their own work schedule. The new position will usually require a minimum of an "8 to 5" work day with the same disciplines imposed on the new sales manager as all other office employees. Although the salesperson often worked more than eight hours per day, the disciplines of the new environment may seem to make the days stretch on forever.

For the first few months, the salesperson may feel like a "duck out of water" while attempting to adjust to the regimented environment of the home office. Most new managers are able to adjust, primarily because their duties still require that they travel in the field on a frequent basis. You can usually see their spirits pick up both before and after a field trip. You can't take the love of the gunfighting out of the Gunfighter. In fact, you don't want to.

Living in a Political Environment

The project salesperson is accustomed to dealing with most issues on an individual basis and "go" or "no-go" decisions are made on the merits of that particular issue. In the home office, many issues cross over departmental boundaries and "territorial rights" can become larger than the issue itself.

Also, the decisions that are being made have greater consequences to the entire organization and are often quite complex. The salesperson in the new position has moved from an individual decision making environment to one that requires committee and group decisions.

153

Politicians understand the need for compromise. The new manager may view differences of opinion as politically motivated. In fact, the discussion may be a normal part of the process in reaching a decision that all departments can live with.

The Salesperson Can Adapt

The above discussion relating to the change in culture that is facing the new sales manager should not infer that they will be unable to adapt . Project salespeople are ''people oriented'' individuals and have highly developed communications skills. Their willingness to adjust to the home office environment is dependent on their commitment to being a successful sales manager. If necessary, the project salesperson has the ability to become a ''chameleon'', if that's what it takes to fit into an environment.

Moving to Another Company

The decision to leave one company and join another should be made for rational, not emotional reasons. The decisions to ''look'' and the possible subsequent decision to ''leap'' should be clearly separated from each other. To ''look'' may be a response to an impulse. To ''leap'' should be the result of a great deal of thought and study. It costs only time to explore alternative career options. But it can cost the salesperson a great deal if the wrong decision is made.

In an earlier chapter we discussed the reasons why a project salesperson is able to make the transition from one company or industry to another without losing their effectiveness. Their aptitudes and skill levels allow them to make changes with relative ease. This is not to imply that they won't have to work hard at acquiring the new product and market knowledge. But, as stated earlier, it is easier to teach this information than it is to develop a person with the ability of the project salesperson.

Reasons for Changing Companies

There are as many reasons why project salespeople change jobs as there are project salespeople. Examples of some of the reasons are shown in figure 3. Most people leave jobs for a combination of reasons, rather than for one specific reason. The primary reasons for project salespeople to change companies is much the same as other people, the desire to move onto a new challenge and to advance their career.

Figure 3.

Reasons for Seeking Alternative Employment

- The company management prefers "flow" over "project" business
- Having been "passed over" for a promotion
- Having to report to a "Farmer" sales manager
- An ongoing disagreement over compensation policies
- Disagreement with company short and long-term direction
- Lack of confidence in company management
- The desire for a new and greater challenge
- Discontinuing or de-emphasizing of "favorite" products
- A desire for career change due to personal reasons
- An untypical lack of fire and drive that they can't explain
- A desire to relocate to another area of the country
- A strong interest in a product or service not offered by their company.
- A feeling that their contribution to the company is not recognized nor appreciated.

Change When the Time is Right for You

It often can require up to a year for the salesperson to find the right match between them and a company. My advice is to never quit a job unless you have another position which has already been offered to you. Incidentally, I haven't always followed this advice. Leaving a job before landing another one places added pressure on the individual to accept a position that may not be ideal. Also, it is easier to find a new job if you are still employed. Prospective employers will know that you do not have to "jump" at the first offer that comes along.

Many compensation and benefits packages have milestone dates attached to pay-outs. Bonus programs often are tied to monthly, quarterly or year end objectives. Profit sharing programs are based on tenure with the company. All of these factors should be considered, but if the right opportunity comes along, the salesperson may decide to forfeit these benefits. The ability of the salesperson to generate an above average income makes these factors less important to them.

What to Look for in a Prospective Company

This depends somewhat on the individual. Figure 4. provides a list of some of the factors that the project salesperson may wish to consider when weighing the benefits of going with one organization over another.

Figure 4.

Factors to Consider in a New Employer

- Does the company and position offer what I am looking for?
- Is the company in the project business? Do they understand it?
- Is the company financially stable?
- What has been their track record for growth and profitability?
- What is the competency level of management?
- Does the company understand its' mission?
- Are there any sales patterns of success established?
- What is the corporate culture? Could I be happy there?
- What are the benefits to me? Compensation, career, etc.
- Who will I report to? Can I work for them?
- What would be the expectations of me?
- Could I develop an emotional tie to the product?
- What are their ethical standards?
- Who are their competitors? Do they understand them?
- Who are their customers? How well do they service them?
- Are they in a stable industry? How fast is it growing?
- What type of salespeople do they currently have?
- What has been the turnover rate for project salespeople?
- Who drives the company? Do they understand the project business?
- Where would I be located? Can my family and I live with that?
- Is this a company I could be proud to work for?

Good project salespeople have little or no problems finding jobs. They develop a successful track record that speaks for itself. They usually have a long list of references, including customers they have worked with. Finding a job is easy, finding the right job can be difficult. The salesperson should take their time and make their selection carefully.

Making the Right Moves

Life is unpredictable and therefore there are no exact right or wrong career decisions. Staying in a position, accepting a promotion, or changing companies are all judgement calls.

It is my opinion that the project salesperson is more valuable having gained experience with at least three companies in their career. All of us become victims of our surroundings and we get locked into certain patterns. This causes us to be narrow in our perspective and limits our effectiveness. The longer an individual works for a company, or with the same group of fellow employees, the more everyone begins to think alike. Adjusting to new environments and working with new people broadens the horizon of the salesperson. I do not mean to infer that the salesperson should change for the sake of change. They should change only if it fits into their intended career path.

Being a project salesperson is an exciting occupation. It provides the professional with a multitude of career options.

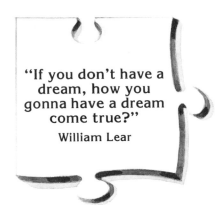

"If you don't have a
dream, how you
gonna have a dream
come true?"
William Lear

CHAPTER FIFTEEN

Bringing it all Together - Realizing Dreams

When I was growing up in Minnesota I remember a saying we used to use when we were going to race each other around the block. One of the gang, hopefully someone not in the race, would say in a loud voice;

> One for the money,
> Two for the show,
> Three to get ready, and...
> Four to go.

This book was written for those in the "three to get ready" and "four to go" categories in their sales career. It is for young sales-people that have high expectations of themselves in their career and for those that are already successful at project selling but recognize that being a professional salesperson requires an on-going commitment to personal development.

Although many salespeople have good intentions, for one reason or another, they never quite get to the "four to go" phase. They dream about success but are never quite willing to make the commitment that is necessary for building a solid foundation. The easiest way to spot them is to look at their sales track records. Being successful at Gunfighter selling means that you've been in competitive battles and won. It also means that you've come away from some gunfights having lost, but gained valuable knowledge.

We Learn More Through Failure than Success

At the risk of trying to sound philosophical, I remember very little about what I learned from those projects that were successful. I can list each of them and I thoroughly enjoyed their pursuit, but no great lessons were learned. On the other hand, I can list every major project that I lost and what I would have done differently if I were given a second chance. Unfortunately, in sales you don't get a second chance on a project, but you can apply what you learned to the next project. In every project that I lost, I was outsold.

When we are successful in getting an order under competitive conditions, we tend to bask in the glory, reflect on how clever we are, and understand very little about the reasons why we were the successful vendor. When we are shattered with the reality that we were beaten by our opponents, we do a great deal more "soul searching" relating to how we should have "done it differently". The salesperson that gets an order rarely asks "why?". The salesperson that loses an order almost always asks "why?".

I believe that this same philosophy has application to many other areas in life. During my sales career I have been promoted on nine occasions to positions that were also being pursued by other individuals. The occasion that I remember most vividly is the promotion that I didn't get. I think I could write a book about that experience. I remember every detail of the process. In retrospect, it was good for me. Incidentally, Denny did a heck of a job in the position.

Winning is Never Final and Losing is Never Fatal

I wonder how many times during my career I've heard the statement ... "well, you can't win them all". This is true, but the ones you don't win hurt. The project salesperson must learn to balance the victories and the defeats and place both of them behind them. The most difficult defeats to handle are those that seem to defy logic. In the selling game, the salesperson rarely sees the entire picture as it has unfolded within the customers organization. I've pursued

160

projects with a great deal of vigor only to learn that one of my competitors was a blood relative to the owner of the company. Incidentally, I've won a few of those.

It's not fun to lose at anything. You show me someone that's consistently a good loser and I'll show you a loser. The important point in selling is that we learn from our mistakes. If you've lost an order, a mistake was made somewhere along the process. Frequently the mistake is made during an early phase of the selling process. One mistake that is frequently made is to not qualify the project sufficiently.

Good Salespeople are Resilient

Surprisingly, it is often as difficult for the salesperson to get back to their selling routines when they have won an order as it is when an order is lost. When a project is over . . . it's over. The resilience that Gunfighters are able to "muster up" often amazes me. If I told you that you just lost the $40,000 equity in your home, I suspect that you would carry that loss with you for the remainder of your life. The project salesperson may face a similar monetary loss on many occasions in their selling career, but they develop a frame of mind which is unique in terms of monetary gain or loss.

The salesperson must look at any loss of monetary gain as if they didn't have the order to begin with and therefore the commission was never earned. The salesperson learns to not . . . "count their chickens before they hatch". Those salespeople that have the toughest time with losing an order are those that start to count their commission or bonus checks before they get the order.

Learning from the Victories and Defeats

One practice that I recommend in the project business is that immediately following the close of an order, write down all of the reasons that you can think of as to why you won or lost the order. This should be done within the first two days that the award is announced. If you are troubled by a loss, ask the customer why you were not the successful vendor. This information should be asked in person, not over the telephone. The salesperson needs more than a voice, they need to read the messages in the eyes and eyebrows.

After several weeks have passed, review your list of the reasons why you won or lost the order. Ask yourself what you would have done differently. Examine areas that you may wish to change in your selling techniques. Then toss the list away. The discarding of the list will help the salesperson to put the win or loss behind them so that they can get on with what they do best . . . selling. The important lessons will be remembered.

Questions and Answers for the Prospective Gunfighter

Rather than providing a review of the book, I have elected to use a "question and answer" format which can be used as a reference for the major points made in the book. This information can be found in the "appendix" of the book located in the last few pages.

Do Dreams Come True?

You bet they do! From the days of our childhood, we dreamed about events or expectations of future happenings. I remember a verse about . . . "visions of sugar plums danced in their heads". I especially like the line used by William Lear . . . "How you gonna have a dream come true if you don't have a dream?"

Project salespeople have a lot of dreams, for themselves, their families and the companies they work for. This book started as a dream and remained that way for many years. In order for most dreams to come true, they have to be translated into goals and objectives. To achieve most goals in life we have to pay some price or dues for our accomplishments.

Paying the Price

In all professional fields, there is an internship or period of testing that must take place before the individual becomes fully competent in their chosen profession. Professionals in all fields; doctors, lawyers, teachers, ministers, etc., must pass through this period. It is a time of trial where dues are paid for future successes. I know of no way to get experience other than to expose oneself to hard work. This internship must also be served by the Gunfighter.

Separating Dreams from Goals

Dreams are dreams. They are fun, pleasant to contemplate and make life interesting but they rarely come true unless they are turned into goals, and an action plan is developed to achieve them. If you wish to become a Gunfighter, establish it as a goal and be willing to pay the price. It will take years of study and self-development. Many individuals have the raw talent, but the moment of truth will come when the prospective Gunfighter comes up against the professional.

In Closing

Best wishes to each of you in your pursuit of a career as a project salesperson. Your future years will be faced with challenging opportunities, and if successful, you will receive a great deal of satisfaction and be rewarded handsomely. Whatever else you do, strive to be recognized as . . . "a professional salesperson". If you can comfortably place that title on your business card, you are a member of a select group.

APPENDIX

Questions and Answers
for Prospective Gunfighters

Question: **What is a Gunfighter?**

Answer: A professional salesperson that is engaged in project sales who has unique natural aptitudes and has developed certain skills that allows them to close large orders and penetrate new accounts.

Question: **Is a Gunfighter made or born?**

Answer: Both. They combine God given abilities with persuasive skills.

Question: **How many Gunfighters are there?**

Answer: Most salespeople believe they are Gunfighters. By my definition, only three percent of the industrial salespeople are Gunfighters. Therefore, there are 36,000 Gunfighters in the United States.

Question: **Can anyone be a Gunfighter?**

Answer: No. They must possess the natural aptitudes. It is estimated that this is one in every fifty-four people. Even if they have the natural aptitudes, they must still develop the necessary skills.

Question: **How would I find out if I had the natural aptitudes?**

Answer: Participate in an aptitude testing program. One such program in the Johnson O'Connor Foundation. This testing will not determine if you are a Gunfighter, but it will determine if you have the aptitudes for selling.

Question: **Does having the natural aptitudes ensure success?**

Answer: No. As Charles Kingsley wrote . . . "He was one of those men who possessed almost every gift, except the gift of the power to use them."

Question: **What is the personality of a Gunfighter?**

Answer: They are high in "wearability". They have a strong "presence", but they are not "over-bearing".

Question: **How would you recognize a Gunfighter?**

Answer: Look at their track record. How many major sales have they closed? It often takes a Gunfighter to recognize a Gunfighter.

Question: **Do the good guys always win?**

Answer: In the long run. In project selling, success cannot be measured in terms of winning or losing one or two orders. Customers have long memories. Integrity and honesty are the trademarks of the Gunfighter.

Question: **Can someone be a Gunfighter without having a mentor?**

Answer: Yes, but it's taking the hard way and it takes longer.

Question: **Where do I find a mentor?**

Answer: You must find each other. A mentor relationship requires mutual consent and agreement. You may feel it and not hear it.

Question: **Does a mentor have to be a boss?**

Answer: No, but it accelerates the process. It provides the opportunity to work on "real" projects.

Question: **Who are other candidates for mentors?**

Answer: Any person that you believe to be a Gunfighter. Start by looking for someone that has had a successful career in selling major projects. A mentor must have a personal interest in your career.

Question: **How long does it take to become a Gunfighter?**

Answer: Sometimes never, sometimes a lifetime. Usually, five to ten years. It depends on the individual, the availability of a mentor and the commitment of the individual.

Question: Is the Gunfighter always successful?

Answer: Success is dependent on the "match" between the Gunfighter and the company they work for.

Question: How does the Gunfighter know when to "hold em" or "fold em"?

Answer: One of the greatest assets of the Gunfighter is their common sense.

Question: Is the Gunfighter an "elitist" theory?

Answer: No. Some people can do some things that others can't.

Question: What skill levels should I work on first?

Answer: All of them, but give special emphasis to communications skills.

Question: If I were a project salesperson, what should I look for in a company?

Answer: An organization that understands and has a commitment to being in the project business.

Question: What type of sales manager is best for my career?

Answer: One that has a proven track record as a project salesperson and is committed to the development of individuals in their sales organizations.

Question: Are Gunfighters "loners"?

Answer: Gunfighters are "team players". They rely on others to ensure their success.

Question: How do I build a team of support people?

Answer: The same way you motivate a thousand people. One at a time.

Question: If I pursue a Gunfighter career, do I have to give up other career options?

Answer: No, but if you become a Gunfighter, you won't want to be anything else. Also, the skills of a Gunfighter apply to many other occupations.

Question: Are all Gunfighters in sales?

Answer: In this book I have coined the term "Gunfighter" to indicate a certain type of salesperson. Many other occupations require similar aptitudes and mental attitudes. Others may be Gunfighters in their chosen fields, but to be a Gunfighter salesperson, the individual must have developed the selling skills and gained project selling experiences.

Question: Can a Gunfighter have a healthy family life?

Answer: You bet! But it is usually best if they have a highly objective spouse that they view as an equal in all matters.

Question: Does the gender of an individual have anything to do with becoming a Gunfighter?

Answer: No, but the majority of the Gunfighters I know happen to be men. I suspect this has to do with experience levels and the past sterotype of salesmen. With more women entering the sales force in project selling, I suspect that many more will be joining the ranks of the Gunfighters. The sex of an individual is immaterial.

Question: If I change companies, do I have to start over?

Answer: The aptitudes and skills that the Gunfighter possesses allows them to change products and industries easily. Their ability to close projects transverses markets.

Question: If it is true that an individuals "greatest strength" is also their "greatest weakness", what would it be for the Gunfighter?

Answer: Impatience.

Question: If I have more questions, would you answer them personally?

Answer: Yes. Send your questions to:
Real Time Strategies
1625 Woodhaven Place
Owatonna, Minnesota 55060.
Please include a self addressed, "stamped" envelope.